Acting Edition

Skeleton Crew

by Dominique Morisseau

D1082586

‖SAMUEL FRENCH‖

ISBN 978-0-573-70516-8

www.concordtheatricals.com
www.concordtheatricals.co.uk

FOR PRODUCTION INQUIRIES

UNITED STATES AND CANADA
info@concordtheatricals.com
1-866-979-0447

UNITED KINGDOM AND EUROPE
licensing@concordtheatricals.co.uk
020-7054-7298

Each title is subject to availability from Concord Theatricals Corp., depending upon country of performance. Please be aware that *SKELETON CREW* may not be licensed by Concord Theatricals Corp. in your territory. Professional and amateur producers should contact the nearest Concord Theatricals Corp. office or licensing partner to verify availability.

This work is published by Samuel French, an imprint of Concord Theatricals Corp.

MUSIC AND THIRD-PARTY MATERIALS USE NOTE

IMPORTANT BILLING AND CREDIT REQUIREMENTS

SKELETON CREW premiered at the Atlantic Theater Company, Stage 2 on January 19, 2016. The performance was directed by Ruben Santiago-Hudson, with scenic design by Michael Carnahan, costume design by Paul Tazewell, lighting design by Rui Rita, original music and sound design by Robert Kaplowitz, original songs by Jimmy "J. Keys" Keys, and chreography by Adesola Osakalumi. The production stage manager was Laura Wilson and the assistant stage manager was Kelly Ice. The cast was as follows:

FAYE .... Lynda Gravatt
DEZ .... Jason Dirden
SHANITA.. Nikiya Mathis
REGGIE................................... Wendell B. Franklin
PERFORMER................................ Adesola Osakalumi

SKELETON CREW was remounted by the Atlantic Theater Company, Linda Gross Theater on May 19, 2016. The performance was directed by Ruben Santiago-Hudson, with scenic design by Michael Carnahan, costume design by Paul Tazewell, lighting design by Rui Rita, original music and sound design by Robert Kaplowitz, original songs by Jimmy "J. Keys" Keys, projections by Nicholas Hussong, and chreography by Adesola Osakalumi. The production stage manager was Laura Wilson. The cast was as follows:

FAYE .... Lynda Gravatt
DEZ .... Jason Dirden
SHANITA.. Nikiya Mathis
REGGIE................................... Wendell B. Franklin
PERFORMER................................ Adesola Osakalumi

SKELETON CREW was developed at the Lark Play Development Center, New York City and the 2014 Sundance Institute Theatre Lab at the Sundance Resort

Winner of the 2014 Sky Cooper New American Play Prize at Marin Theatre Company, Mill Valley, CA, Artistic Director, Jasson Minadakis; Managing Director, Michael Barker

CHARACTERS

FAYE – Black woman, mid-to-late fifties. Working-class woman. Tough and a lifetime of dirt beneath her nails. Somewhere, deep compassion.

DEZ – Black man, mid-to-late twenties. Working-class young man. Young hustler, playful, street-savy, and flirtatious. Somewhere, deeply sensitive.

SHANITA – Black woman, mid-to-late twenties. Working-class young woman. Pretty but not ruled by it. Hard-working. By-the-books. Believes in the work she does. Also, pregnant. Somewhere, a beautiful dreamer.

REGGIE – Black man, late thirties. White-collar man. Studious. Dedicated. Compassionate. The Foreman. Somewhere, a fire brims.

SETTING

Detroit, Michigan. Stamping Plant. Winter.

TIME

Somewhere around year 2008.

AUTHOR'S NOTES

This play operates in realism with touches of the magical/ethereal. The moments where the mechanical intrusion of the story peeks into the transitions should not feel like cool tricks separate from the base of the play. They are part of the storytelling of automation. They are part of the omnipresence of the plant without overwhelming the realism of the play. I guess simply put, my ask would be however your production imagines this automation (shadow puppets, choreography, video, a combo of all), that it doesn't become a shtick, but instead continues to add to the fullness of the plant so that even though we're only seeing the breakroom, we're also seeing the whole factory deteriorating.

The language of the play must also drive. These characters have a banter with each other that is so natural and second nature that they can almost finish each other's sentences. As much as possible, breaks or pauses between text or within passages of text should be avoided until written in. There are silences in the ellipses or pauses that are written into the text such that they make an impact.

This is for my Auntie Francine, my grandfather Pike, my cousins Michael Abney and Patti Poindexter, my Uncle Sandy, my friend David Livingston, my relative Willie Felder, and all of the UAW members and auto workers whose passion for their work inspires me. And this is for the working class warriors who keep this country driving forward.

This is also for the politicians, financial analysts, and everyday citizens who echoed the negating sentiments, "Let Detroit Go Bankrupt." Yep, this is for you too, damnit.

ACT ONE

Scene One

(In darkness, smoke comes out of a stack. The sound of auto plant machinery hums and rattles. Hip-hop drum beats [J Dilla-inspired] blend into the rhythm – a cacophony of working class hustle. Echos of sighs. Machinery hums hums hums. J Dilla-inspired beats rock rock rock. They blend together until we are almost bopping our heads to it...a factory line hymn...)

(In silhouette – the drone of workers on the line. Actions of operating stamping machinery. No clear people. Just shadowed workers misted by the smoke.)

(The background sounds fade out.)

(Lights rise on the breakroom at a stamping plant. Harsh fluorescent lights bleach the room. Posters on the wall of various cars and SUVs. Pictures of various auto parts – shocks, sparking engines, etc.)

(A table and some chairs sit in the middle of the room. A raggedy couch. Some crates that hold random kitchen supplies – plasticware, ketchup packets, etc.)

(Somewhere, a microwave and refrigerator.)

(Most important in the room: the bulletin board. Covered in notices and papers. But larger than them all are two signs, posted on top and in bigger paper.)

(One, handwritten, says "Unit Meeting THURSDAY. Don't Miss It Again Ya'll.")

(The other, also handwritten, says "NO SMOKING FAYE.")

*(**FAYE**, heavy walk and weathered from the day, walks into the breakroom. Over to her locker. Takes off a sweatshirt, leaving her in a white t-shirt and hard yellow boots. Dirty and worn. She moves past the "No Smoking" sign. Looks at it blankly.)*

(Pulls out a cigarette from her bosom. Lights it and puffs.)

*(**DEZ** enters, wearing gloves and a vest.)*

DEZ. Cold then a bitch today, ain't it?

FAYE. *(Puffing.)* Shiiitt.

DEZ. Told them fools something ain't right with the heat in here. Upstairs could give a damn less.

FAYE. Reggie bringing in a heater today, supposed to.

DEZ. Reggie supposed to been brought in a heater – days ago. Head somewhere else.

FAYE. He got a lot on his mind lately.

DEZ. He ain't the only one.

*(**DEZ** opens the fridge. Pulls out a lunch. Dilapidated sandwich. Looks at it pitifully. Bites into it anyway. Looks at **FAYE** squarely.)*

You ain't cold?

FAYE. I got a heat you don't know shit about. Leave me 'lone.

DEZ. *(Laughing.)* Awww hell Faye. You on that over-fifty pause?

FAYE. You better leave me 'lone – talking 'bout over-fifty.

DEZ. You hittin' my mama status. It's 'bout to get serious.

FAYE. I told you don't mess with me boy.

DEZ. I know how ya'll do. Be in the dead of winter, and she talkin' 'bout – "Dez, roll the car window down." I'm like – hell naw, Ma! Why I gotta freeze in the middle of January just cuz you in yo' own personal July?

FAYE. I hope yo' mama slapped you good. Ain't 'spose to bother a woman battlin' her own heat.

DEZ. You know you ain't supposed to be smokin'. You ain't see Reggie's sign?

FAYE. This what I think of Reggie's sign.

(She blows a circle of smoke.)

DEZ. You know he gon' trip. Can write you up.

FAYE. Bet' not.

DEZ. You think you a O-G, don't you?

FAYE. I'm is, fool. Been on the line longer than you been born.

DEZ. You swear.

FAYE. 'Fore you knocked up yo' first girlfriend in the back of somebody's Ford.

DEZ. You know I ain't never knocked up nobody in no nothin'.

FAYE. Been puttin' in my time 'fore you even knew what a stamping plant was, fool. I'm yo' elder up in here. Bow down and lick the dust off my Tims.

DEZ. You better go'on somewhere with that.

*(The door to the breakroom opens. **SHANITA**, a young woman wearing goggles, enters. She is visibly pregnant. She heads straight for the fridge.)*

*(**DEZ** smiles at her.)*

Hey baby.

SHANITA. Shut up Dez.

FAYE. She gone' file a sexual harassment report on yo' tail. And I'ma throw the book at you.

DEZ. Psshhhh…

SHANITA. Who had some of my salad dressing?

DEZ. Wasn't me.

FAYE. Me neither.

SHANITA. I put my name on it. Big letters – S-H-A-N-I-T-A. Who the hell can't read?

(She sits down in a huff and tends to her salad.)

FAYE. Ya'll and these damn signs.

DEZ. What you eatin' salad for? I like my women with meat on their bones.

SHANITA. Boy you swear to somebody's god that I want you. *(Shift.)* Faye, you smokin' in here?

FAYE. For five seconds.

SHANITA. Ahem!

(**SHANITA** *indicates her pregnant belly.*)

FAYE. I'm sorry I'm sorry.

(**FAYE** *puts out the cig.*)

Shit. Ya'll the ones invadin' my lil' hideaway. Ain't nobody stopping you from eatin' in yo' cars with the rest of them fools. *(Mumbling.)* Worryin' 'bout me 'steada all that dust out there swimming in yo' lungs.

SHANITA. I wear my mask. And I'm not stepping off the line until I absolutely have to. Get the most of my benefits. *(Shift.)* Thought you quit, anyway.

FAYE. That patch is a damn lie. All these programs are. You quit when you're ready to quit. 'Til then, you just a nicotine tease. Flirt with her 'til you kiss her right down to the ash.

SHANITA. You better quit, Faye. Don't know nobody that invincible they can battle breast cancer and still be smokin' like it ain't no thang.

DEZ. Faye like flirtin' with death.

FAYE. Been this way over fifty years, don't see why I gotta change now.

SHANITA. What's your son got to say about that?

FAYE. Not a damn thing.

SHANITA. Stubborn.

DEZ. As a mule.

FAYE. Ya mamas. *(Shift.)* How's production comin' on the three-line?

SHANITA. Slow. Since we done lost half the crew, I don't know how Reggie expect us to meet deadline. I'm already workin' overtime four days this week. My feet swellin' as it is.

DEZ. Want me to rub 'em?

SHANITA. Want me to kick you?

FAYE. I'll take yo' overtime. And Dez too, if you want.

DEZ. Not me, naw. You know I'm saving up.

FAYE. You still talkin' 'bout starting that repair shop?

DEZ. Found me a garage over on six mile. All I gotta do is save me enough to buy it outright. Few more months of overtime, I'm in there.

FAYE. And then what? You quit?

DEZ. You mean if we ain't next to get dropped? It's dead flies all around this plant, Faye. I ain't waitin' 'round 'til I get swat.

FAYE. Anywhere else you go you get swat there too, shit. Ain't nothin' new.

SHANITA. You got to make yourself irreplaceable. That's what I'm doing.

FAYE. How you figure you irreplaceable? I been from stamping doors to installing shocks to them seven years I spent sewing interiors. It ain't nobody in this plant more irreplaceable than Faye Davison.

SHANITA. I'm talking work efficiency and ethic. I don't complain. Got the least write-ups. Do a lotta overtime.

DEZ. And you fine then a mug *(as in "muthafucker")*. That make you irreplaceable as hell to me.

SHANITA. And that's sexual harassment number 5,062.

DEZ. I notice you keepin' count.

SHANITA. And anyway, I'm in good standing with the union.

FAYE. Everybody in good standin' with the union, except for Dez.

DEZ. Dues too damn much.

FAYE. You youngins don't have no respect for the blood been spilled so yo' ass have some benefits.

DEZ. What benefits? I don't hardly see no benefits.

FAYE. Was a time when you wasn't even allowed in the union, dummy. Wasn't nothin' but the mule of the industry doin' the shittiest labor you could think of. And now here you are, *choosing* yo' trade and thinkin' you got that shit all by yo'self.

DEZ. Faye don't start all that with me. You bastards pull money outta my paycheck every month, for what? Only thing the UAW do for me is force me to strike when I don't even want to. Rather stack my paper and build my own enterprise. I done paid enough dues in my life already, I ain't tryin' to pay to nobody else. Them union suckers might get my money, but I ain't got to smile and grin while I sign the shit over. I feel like grittin' my teeth, I'm grittin' my teeth.

FAYE. You ain't seen no UAW strikes 'til you done lost a few teeth to assholes trying to break yo' line and fight you down into the gutter. I can always demonstrate upside yo' head if you need to know how it went.

SHANITA. Knock him out real good, Faye.

DEZ. Awww baby, you ain't got to knock me out. You can just have your way with me.

SHANITA. Boy please.

> (*The door to the breakroom opens.* **REGGIE**, *Black man with neat haircut, neat pants, and a white-collar button-down shirt, enters. He rolls in a heater.*)

REGGIE. Faye, there you are. I was looking for you.

FAYE. For what? I still got a half hour left to my break. Tell them fools on sixteen-line to take a chill pill and let me rest my dogs.

REGGIE. Wanted to chat with you for a sec.

SHANITA. Finally, a heater!

REGGIE. Smell like smoke in here.

SHANITA. You know who that was.

REGGIE. How big I got to make the sign?

FAYE. Bigger.

DEZ. You got more overtime for me?

REGGIE. I might be able to find something. But Charlie and Bo put in before you.

DEZ. Charlie and Bo been gettin' overtime all week. What about me?

REGGIE. What about you? You want me to throw them to the side cuz you took too long to ask?

DEZ. Don't mean you gotta let them have all the overtime. Ain't 'spose to be no monopolies on overtime.

REGGIE. Don't start fussing with me Dez. I don't need your insubordination today.

DEZ. Insubordination?

SHANITA. Dez can have my overtime. I was gonna tell you anyway. Had to take a doctor's appointment this afternoon. Only time I could get in.

FAYE. Gonna find out the gender?

SHANITA. Not sure yet. Think I wanna be surprised.

REGGIE. Fine. Dez, you're on. I'm done with it. *(Shift.)* I'm gonna plug this up, but then you ain't gonna be able to use the microwave. Can't use too much wattage in this outlet. Gonna have to pick and choose.

DEZ. If that ain't hood-rigging, I don't know what is.

REGGIE. Gotta take what we can get.

FAYE. That's a company heater? Or you brought that from home?

REGGIE. Just take the heater.

FAYE. Foremen ain't responsible for bringing in personal heaters to keep the breakroom warm.

REGGIE. Just take the heater.

DEZ. Ay Reggie, I heard they closed down Kemp.

REGGIE. Where'd you hear that?

DEZ. Bony J.

REGGIE. News from Bony J always comes crooked and on the diagonal. You know not to listen to rumors like that.

DEZ. Nah nah, he showed it to me in Plant Closing News.

SHANITA. It's in the newsletter?

DEZ. Think I'm lyin'?

REGGIE. I guess they went on ahead with it then. Thought they got revived when that new Chrysler came out. Kemp was the number one company for exporting their shocks.

DEZ. They doin' 'em within now.

SHANITA. That make us the last small factory standing now, ain't it?

FAYE. Shoul do.

REGGIE. That sixteen-line is gonna be a massive undertaking. They gonna have to bring in rigging crews from all over. If you start hittin' the gym more Dez, you can go'on down there and find you some pickup work.

DEZ. Psshhhh – too bad I could give a damn less watching another plant turn into a ghost-town. I'm straight on that.

FAYE. You 'fraid of ghosts?

DEZ. Them assembly line ghosts? Hell yeah.

SHANITA. Shut up, Dez.

DEZ. Say them empty plants a breeding ground for 'em. You can hear the echoes of machines just runnin' and runnin' in the hollow space. Them fools that be goin' down there playin' in the ruins; dumb-ass White boys come over from Windsor and Ohio to stand in front of those empty plants and take pictures like it's some kinda cabaret step and repeat? Heard that be the last picture they ever take. Some of them jokers never make it back out. The old gas vapors swallow them whole. Disappear.

SHANITA. That's stupid.

REGGIE. Even more stupid is the press operator that goes around spreading that mess.

DEZ. You ain't got to believe me. I know what I know.

FAYE. And that ain't much.

DEZ. *(Checking his watch.)* Shit, my break almost over and I ain't even get to make good on my promise to Bony J. 'Sposed to catch him for a game of bones and take his money right quick.

REGGIE. You know you're not supposed to gamble on work grounds. I could write you up.

DEZ. You got to catch me in action first.

> *(DEZ heads to the door.)*

See ya'll at quittin' time. Shanita, I'll meet you out front to walk you to your car. Ain't safe out there after dark.

SHANITA. You hit on me and I'm gonna pepper spray your ass.

DEZ. Not 'til our first date, baby.

> *(SHANITA throws something nearby at DEZ. Maybe a styrofoam cup. He disappears behind the door.)*

SHANITA. I'ma go back too. Still got ten minutes, but I'm walkin' slow these days. Swollen feet ain't quick feet, you know? *(Shift.)* Hey Faye, I'm bringing in a book of names tomorrow. You gonna help me pick somethin'?

FAYE. Thought you said you didn't wanna know the gender.

SHANITA. Somethin' unisex.

> *(SHANITA leaves. FAYE watches REGGIE as he straightens things up. A moment of awkwardness.)*

REGGIE. Was um…lookin' for you cuz I needed to talk…if you had a sec.

> *(FAYE eyes REGGIE intensely.)*

FAYE. *(Not a question.)* They shuttin' us down, ain't they.

REGGIE. How you –

FAYE. I know you Reggie. Can read your face. Been lookin' stressed for a week and then some. *(Beat.)* When you find out?

REGGIE. Last week. Harris pulled me into his office.

FAYE. Fuck.

>   *(Pause.)*

When they letting everybody know?

REGGIE. HR is sending out the notice as soon details are final.

FAYE. How soon this happenin'?

REGGIE. Within the year, Faye.

FAYE. *(Sobering.)* FUCK.

>   *(Another pause.)*

I hit thirty years at the end of the year. In October. We gonna be around that long?

REGGIE. Ain't sure.

FAYE. *(Almost to herself.)* Retirement package be real different for twenty-nine years versus thirty.

REGGIE. I know. I'm thinking on it. Was coming to talk to you. Get the scoop on folks. See what I might be able to figure out for everybody before the news hits. Cuz once it does...

FAYE. What you gonna do? What about Cheryl and the kids?

REGGIE. I've been trying to figure that out. I only got fifteen years on me.

FAYE. But you in a supervisory position. They gonna find you another job. Place you somewhere else.

REGGIE. Dalina just started high school. Got to save up for her college. And we just bought that house over in Sherwood. Couldn't hardly believe we could afford it. But we got it, Faye. It's ours.

FAYE. I know it.

REGGIE. I own something that can't nobody take from me. That mean somethin'.

FAYE. It does. Means a lot.

REGGIE. Now you can't say nothin' about this. I'll lose my job. You know that right?

FAYE. I know you don't expect me to sit on this. That's not what you was coming to ask me.

REGGIE. I was coming for your help. To work with you and figure out what we can do to soften this blow. But you can't go taking this to the union yet. I need you to wait and let the company do this right.

FAYE. Do this right? Only right way is straight up. I'm still the rep. It's my job to protect these folks.

REGGIE. Faye, I'm confiding in you. I'm putting myself on the line for you cuz I'm on your side. But I need you on mine. I need your guidance. Help me figure this out without sounding the alarm.

FAYE. Reggie –

REGGIE. Please Faye.

> (FAYE *says nothing.*)

I wouldn't be in this industry if it wasn't for you. My mama never stopped reminding me that, you know. You always been her most trusted soul sister. Recommended me to get a good job in the factory when wasn't nobody hiring a high school dropout. And now look. I'm wearing a tie to work and buying a house for my family. *(Beat.)* I always appreciate that, Faye. You know that, right?

FAYE. *(Softly.)* I know it. She'd be real proud of you.

REGGIE. I'm gonna work hard to get us outta here with somethin' we can exhale into. Just please…until I can figure this out…

FAYE. Alright, Reggie. Fine. We'll do it your way.

> (REGGIE *stares at* FAYE *for a moment. Releases a smile.*)

REGGIE. Thanks Faye. You tough as bricks, you know that? Ain't nothin' can knock you down.

FAYE. See you in the mornin'.

REGGIE. Alright then.

> (REGGIE *heads to the door.*)

And leave those cigarettes alone Faye. If not for the plant rules, at least for your health. Jalen would kill

me if he knew I let his mama smoke herself out of
remission.

FAYE. My son ain't givin' two shits 'bout that. *(Shift.)* Get
outta here. I'll see you in the morning.

REGGIE. See you then.

> (**REGGIE** *exits.* **FAYE** *stands still after him for a
> moment.)*
>
> *(Then she reaches into her bosom. Pulls out another
> cigarette. Lights it.)*
>
> *(And puffs…)*

Scene Two

(In darkness, the humming of machinery creates a midwest hip-hop score. It is an extension of the factory line soundtrack that opened the play.)

(Silhouetted workers are seen in action – their factory line dance.)

(Suddenly, a chink in the machinery. The workers repeat movements as if they are stuck between two motions – unable to complete their task. Short circuiting – caught in dysfunction.)

(Lights crossfade onto the breakroom.)

(It is early morning. Sunlight spills into the windows. Clothes are lying around on the floor and the dilapidated couch. A locker is partially open. The heater is on.)

(DEZ enters the breakroom wearing a coat and backpack. Walks over to a boombox resting on a crate. Unplugs the heater and plugs in the boombox. Puts on a CD. Slum Village, "Get Dis Money."*)

(Notices the clothes that are lain about. The open locker. Registers it questionably.)

(Takes out his hard boots. Changes out of his nice gym shoes. Puts gym shoes in locker. Takes off backpack. Looks around himself. Pulls a gun from his hip. Places it in his backpack and seals it good.)

---

* A license to produce *SKELETON CREW* does not include a performance license for "Get Dis Money" by Slum Village. The publisher and author suggest that the licensee contact ASCAP or BMI to ascertain the music publisher and contact such music publisher to license or acquire permission for performance of the song. If a license or permission is unattainable for "Get Dis Money," the licensee may not use the song in *SKELETON CREW* but may create an original composition in a similar style. For further information, please see music use note on page 3.

(Pulls out lunch, takes it over to fridge. Opens fridge and sticks head in, looking for something to drink. Shakes OJ cartons, smells milk, etc.)

(SHANITA enters, yawning. Walks right over to the boombox and turns it off.)

(SHANITA goes to her locker and takes off her coat. Stores her belongings. Puts some new salad dressing in the fridge.)

DEZ. *(Rapidly.)* Whoa whoa whoa what up doe? Why you turnin' off my music?

SHANITA. It's too early for this.

DEZ. Morning ritual. I'm sayin'. You messin' up my mojo. Slum Village is my muse.* Make me feel like gettin' my hustle on.

SHANITA. I'm being selective about what I listen to while I'm pregnant. Only positive sounds for my baby to hear.

DEZ. What's more positive than makin' that paper?

SHANITA. Seriously, Dez. Mother-to-be. I get priority.

DEZ. A'ight, what you wanna hear? I got other stuff.

SHANITA. Silence. The sound of the refrigerator humming. The sound of the machines running. That's it.

DEZ. That ain't music.

SHANITA. To you, maybe not. To me, it is. Sound like harmony. Like life happening. Production. Good sound.

DEZ. I'm still pissed they busted me for playin' music on the floor. My mind goes numb listening to that stamping sound all day long. A dude could forget how to socialize with the outside world. Forget how to lay that pimp game down on a woman. Got nobody to practice with.

SHANITA. Don't think you 'bout to practice with me.

---

* "Slum Village is my muse" is an optional line and should be spoken by Dez only if licensees have acquired performance rights to "Get Dis Money" by Slum Village.

DEZ. Who else I'm 'sposed to practice with? Faye? That's like hittin' on my Aunt Debra. You the finest woman up in this plant.

SHANITA. What am I – your default hottie? No thank you.

DEZ. You know you more than that to me.

SHANITA. Whatever.

> *(Beat.)*

DEZ. Yo' baby daddy brought you here this mornin'?

SHANITA. Do not ask me about my child's father. Not up for discussion Dez.

DEZ. My bad –

SHANITA. You like pissin' me off early in the morning?

DEZ. You look cute when you pissed off. Got that pregnancy glow.

> *(She fumes at him. He backs off.)*

A'ight. Too early for compliments I guess.

SHANITA. You don't know what a compliment is, I guess.

> *(DEZ makes himself busy in the makeshift kitchen.)*

DEZ. You want some coffee?

SHANITA. One cup. Milk –

DEZ. And two sugars. I know. I got you.

> *(SHANITA folds the clothes.)*

SHANITA. Who came in here earlier than us? That's Faye stuff?

DEZ. Yeah.

SHANITA. You heard them rumors down on nine-line yesterday?

DEZ. I heard 'em.

SHANITA. Think it's true?

DEZ. Bet' not be. I still got about six months left 'fore I have enough for my garage.

SHANITA. But what if they are?

DEZ. Can't stress over that. Rumors 'bout shuttin' down been circulating every year. Then it go away. That's just how it is. Can't worry 'bout it. Cuz if it don't happen, you done worried for nothin'. And if it do happen, you done worried twice. Better to wait to the last possible moment to start worryin', I say. 'Til then, just sit back and go with the flow.

SHANITA. Yo' philosophies be…

DEZ. Stupid?

SHANITA. Halfway comforting…

> *(Beat.* **DEZ** *hands* **SHANITA** *a cup of coffee. They sip in silence. The sound of the refrigerator runs.* **SHANITA** *closes her eyes.)*

DEZ. I wasn't sayin' nothin' about yo' baby's daddy. Just wanted to know –

SHANITA. Shhhhh…Listen to the music.

> *(***DEZ** *watches her…kinda smiles…)*
>
> *(Beat.)*
>
> *(***FAYE** *walks in – startled at the sight of them.)*

FAYE. Oh – hey…ya'll ain't usually here this early.

DEZ. You in a lil' early yourself, ain't you?

> *(***FAYE** *averts* **DEZ**'s *eyes. Goes to grab her clothes.)*

FAYE. Forgive my mess…

> *(***FAYE** *puts the clothes away. Shuts her locker.)*

SHANITA. You made the coffee?

FAYE. Yeah.

SHANITA. Taste a lil' different.

DEZ. Better than this slop we usually drink.

FAYE. Brought some of my own beans in. Gourmet coffee beans or some shit. Christmas gift from my son. Ain't got no coffee maker, but he don't know that. So figured I might as well share 'fore they go to waste or whatever.

SHANITA. That's cool Faye, thanks.

FAYE. Whatever. Better than wasting 'em. *(Shift.)* Who workin' overtime tonight?

SHANITA. I'm gonna. Put in my request yesterday.

DEZ. Not me. I got a date.

SHANITA. A date?

DEZ. Yeah. Why – you jealous?

SHANITA. *(A little.)* Pssshhhhh…

FAYE. What you gonna take her out in? Not that hooptie you got out there.

DEZ. Hooptie?

FAYE. So much rust on that car – look like it got a disease. Lesions everywhere.

DEZ. You talk shit now, but I'm 'bout to be working on her. She gonna look real pretty in a couple of months. Ain't gonna hardly be able to recognize her.

FAYE. Ya'll youngins don't know nothin' 'bout how to fix up no car. Treat 'em 'bout as dumb as you treat women. Put a bunch of pretty jewelry on her – gold rims – trick out her exterior and on the inside, she ain't got nothin' to run on. No care. No substance. Just put all your attention on the shit that don't matter. That ain't how to make her purr like you really want.

DEZ. Like you know somethin' –

FAYE. I know how to get a girl in the back of my car faster than you. Tell you that much.

SHANITA. Faye be mackin' the ladies.

FAYE. I ain't said I be mackin' 'em. I just said I know how. If it's one thing I always known, it's cars and women. I keep all of it in tact better than Dez keep his. Bet you that.

DEZ. I keep my cars and my women tight. Don't worry 'bout that.

FAYE. That ol' Betsie you drive ain't got nothin' to run on. Engine sound like it's gonna die on you any day now. Like a ol' dirty woman with a emphysema cough. Hear that girl hacking for her life everytime you drive in the lot. Mile away.

DEZ. You gon' be that ol' dirty woman you keep smokin' –

FAYE. Hush that.

DEZ. Anyway, I'm fixin' to get a new engine. Got the hook up.

SHANITA. Where – at one of them auctions? Heard they for big ol' press machines. Cranes and lifts and whatever. Where you gettin' a new engine?

DEZ. My boy work over at the Briggs Plant. Said he gonna hold one off to the side for me.

FAYE. That sound like some sideways and upside down shit to me. You better be careful dealin' with yo' boy. Police already arrested two fools last week for stealing plant materials.

Happenin' a whole bunch right now. Some of those ol' dusty ghost towns you talk about are getting ransacked. Poppy Johnson – the nightwatchman over at Kemps – got himself shot in the shoulder one night while he was patroling the grounds. Didn't even get no disabilty.

SHANITA. Plants ain't safe no more.

FAYE. Nowhere safe no more. Everybody packin' somethin' these days. Can't go to the corner store without worryin' whether the person you blocked in is gonna come gunnin' at you cuz they got someplace to be in a hurry. Use to be able to offend somebody without losin' your life as the cost...

DEZ. How the hell else they 'spose to go around? Unarmed? You can't coast this city that way 'less you suicidal.

SHANITA. Why can't you? I do. I don't need my baby to come into this world armed and dangerous.

FAYE. Everybody handle tension differently. Some folks see shit fallin' apart and got to join in the destruction. Hands with no use find activity in useless shit. But some folks think on a different plane. Rather be part of the restoration. And some folks just...

SHANITA. What?

FAYE. Smoke a goddamn cigarette. *(Shift.)* Where my pack?

> (DEZ *holds up an empty pack.*)

DEZ. You out.

FAYE. Hell, I got to go and get me some. Or you can get me a pack on your lunch break.

DEZ. I'll think about it. Don't know if I wanna be part of your destruction.

FAYE. Boy, I'll slap you.

SHANITA. Faye, you heard them rumors flying 'round the plant lately?

FAYE. What rumors?

SHANITA. Say we next on the choppin' block?

FAYE. Told you don't be listening to rumors. You inhale every rumor you clog up your lungs. Die of asphyxiation of other people's bullshit.

DEZ. I'm gonna get to the bottom of all that hearsay.

FAYE. How you figure that?

DEZ. Gonna ask Reggie straight out. He know somethin' and he ain't tellin' us? That's bitch-made to me.

FAYE. You back offa Reggie. Got himself a lot to deal with already. Counselin' all kinda folks losing they jobs. Ain't easy.

SHANITA. But he gotta tell us, right? I need to keep my benefits.

FAYE. *(Changing the subject.)* Shanita, I almost forgot – I got somethin' for you.

> (FAYE *goes to her locker. Pulls out a stack of paper.*
> *Hands it to* SHANITA.)

SHANITA. What's this?

FAYE. List of names. Unisex.

SHANITA. For real?

FAYE. Printed 'em at the computer in Bea's old office. Go on look at 'em.

SHANITA. *(Reading aloud.)* African baby names.

DEZ. Awww hell – African names? That kid ain't gonna be able to get no job.

SHANITA. Shut up Dez!

FAYE. You a special kinda stupid.

SHANITA. *(Reading.)* Akia.

FAYE. Yeah, I like that one. Means "first born."

DEZ. What kinda significance is that? That's like naming a kid – Born On Wednesday.

SHANITA. *(Reading.)* That's Akua.

FAYE. Got significance, fool. Days of week mean things to some people.

SHANITA. Wednesday mean something to me. Means a longer workday. Means being just like my daddy. Mean a lot.

DEZ. *(Regretfully.)* I ain't sayin' it don't mean nothin'.

> *(Beat. SHANITA checks her watch.)*

SHANITA. It's almost nine o'clock. Gotta get on the floor.

> *(She raises to her feet. FAYE grabs a nearby deck of cards.)*

FAYE. Who got time for a game of Spades before the bell? Dez, lemme take your money right quick.

DEZ. Not me, nah. I already lost a bill yesterday. I'm off gambling today.

FAYE. Come back on break. Maybe you have a change of heart. Need me somewhere to play…keep my mind off shit.

DEZ. Off what?

FAYE. Just shit.

> *(SHANITA heads to the door.)*

SHANITA. I'll be back at break Faye. I'll play you. *(Shift.)* And don't let nobody take my salad dressing.

> *(SHANITA exits.)*
>
> *(DEZ clears the table.)*

FAYE. I got that.

DEZ. Nah, I do. Let me.

> (DEZ *throws coffee cups away. Stops. Looks at* FAYE *for a moment.*)

FAYE. *(Not a question.)* What.

DEZ. You...alright?

FAYE. I'm fine. What's your deal?

DEZ. The clothes –

FAYE. I'm fine. What's your deal?

DEZ. Nothing. I guess.

> *(Pause. Silence.)*

I ain't gonna say nothin', but –

FAYE. Then don't.

DEZ. But the shit is concerning.

FAYE. Let it go, Dez.

DEZ. If Reggie find out –

FAYE. If Reggie find out what? Reggie ain't finding out nothin'. Reggie ain't finding out about my clothes lain around or me being here when ya'll arrived this morning. Reggie ain't finding out about me gambling on the premises. And Reggie ain't findin' out about that gun you keep in your locker. Right? Reggie ain't findin' nothin' out.

DEZ. How you –

FAYE. I know everything about this place, Dez. The walls talk to me. The dust on the floors write me messages. I'm in the vents. I'm in the bulletin boards. I'm in the chipped paint. Ain't nobody can slip through the cracks past me up in here. I can see through lockers. I know what you got in that bag you bring in here everyday. But I don't expose it. Cuz everybody got they bag of shit. You got yours. And I got mine. Leave me to my own stink and don't go tryin' to air me out.

DEZ. What if we just worried about you?

FAYE. Worry 'bout that car need fixin'. Worry 'bout that darkness out there that make you afraid to coast without that metal. But don't worry 'bout me. I'm just fine.

>*(Beat.)*

DEZ. Alright.

>**(DEZ** *grabs a pair of goggles and heads to the door.)*

I'll come back with your poison at break.

FAYE. I'll come back here lookin' for it...

>**(DEZ** *exits.)*

>**(FAYE** *stands alone for a moment.)*

>*(Looks around the room. Sighs. And exits.)*

Scene Three

(Lights rise on **REGGIE** *in the breakroom. He is putting up signs on the bulletin board.)*

(First sign reads: "THEFT ALERT. Materials Missing. If you see something, Contact Supervisor." Second sign reads: "No Gambling on Premises. Dez, this means YOU.")

*(***DEZ*** enters the breakroom. Sees* **REGGIE**. *Sees sign. Rolls his eyes and goes over to his locker.)*

DEZ. *(Under his breath.)* Here we go.

REGGIE. Don't start with me Dez.

DEZ. It's like 100 less trees in the world cuz of all the paper you use to cover this board. Can't you just spare us all and say what you got to say?

REGGIE. I say it and you don't listen. But you better start listening real soon. Things are changing around here.

DEZ. Oh yeah? How so?

REGGIE. Plant was hit last night.

DEZ. Say word?

REGGIE. Took us for a good eighth of sheet metal off the thirteen-line.

DEZ. No kiddin'?

REGGIE. That's right. Upstairs is cracking down on all improper conduct on the floor. That means playing dominoes with Bony J. That means everything Dez.

DEZ. What does me playin' bones have to do with the plant gettin' robbed?

REGGIE. They're losing patience. Zero tolerance policy for any criminal activity on the premises.

DEZ. They got a zero tolerance policy for the criminal activity happening upstairs? Or does that street only run one way.

REGGIE. Cool it with the backtalk, Dez. I told you don't start with me today. I say cut out the gambling, that's what I mean. And whatever else you like to do in opposition to company protocol.

DEZ. I ain't got to move in opposition of nothin'. I understand the rules real clear, Boss.

REGGIE. Good.

> (*Beat.* REGGIE *sighs. Continues to post signs on the board.* "Unit Meeting Thursday." "Keep The Breakroom Clean." "No Personal Items Left In The Breakroom After Hours.")

DEZ. Speaking of protocol...

REGGIE. What of it?

DEZ. Folks startin' to talk on the shop floor.

REGGIE. Folks always talk on the shop floor. What of it?

DEZ. Sayin' this plant might be the next one to turn into a ghost town. Sound like HR is about to have a whole bunch of shit on they hands. Ain't that right?

REGGIE. I'm not speaking on hearsay.

DEZ. What you mean you not speakin' on it? Either it's happening or it's not.

REGGIE. What are you getting so concerned about HR for? You can barely focus on the line you're working on – why you worrying about HR?

DEZ. Cuz I wanna hear you say it. Tell us the plant is closing down and what we gotta do to make sure we get covered right.

REGGIE. You want me to tell you something that I can't.

DEZ. You can't, hunh?

REGGIE. What do you want from me, Dez? Didn't I just say I don't have nothin' to tell you? The company hasn't folded yet. You just focus on your job and keep your stat sheet clean, and stop worrying about things nobody can control right now.

DEZ. Can't control? Or don't wanna deal with?

REGGIE. You got something you wanna say to me directly? Or you gonna keep grabbing at stuff in the air without landing on nothing. Because I already told you what to do if you wanna make sure you're covered. Do your job. Lay off the disorderly conduct. And stay out of the shop room gossip. It doesn't suit you well.

DEZ. It doesn't suit me well?

REGGIE. No.

DEZ. What is it with you lately, man?

REGGIE. There's nothing with me.

DEZ. Act like you ain't come up in here the same way the rest of us did. The color of that collar don't change yo' origins. You forget that?

REGGIE. *(Getting heated.)* Don't question my collar, Dez.

DEZ. Ain't questioning the collar. Questioning the man wearin' it.

REGGIE. You question me again and I'll show you exactly what my origins are. I'm done being pushed this way and that, while you completely disrespect my position.

DEZ. Faye got you that position.

REGGIE. Who cares who got me the position?! I'm in it. And I'm your supervisor. And I'm telling you this as clear as I can think to say it…if I catch you doing one thing out of line anywhere on these premises, I will carry out the orders I've been given. And that's not just a write-up this time. It's not even suspension. It's the law. They're pressing charges to anyone stepping over the line. You understand that? That's charges Dez. And you can push back at me and say whatever slick comment that comes out of your mouth, but it's not going to change a damn thing. You break the law, you're done.

(**FAYE** *enters the breakroom.*)

FAYE. What's all this heat about in here? The radiator broken? Ya'll trying to create yo' own?

(**DEZ** *fumes.* **REGGIE** *turns away and grabs his materials.*)

Hey Reggie, you alright there? Need to talk for a minute?

REGGIE. Need to get back upstairs.

FAYE. You wanna come talk later?

REGGIE. Can't. Dalina got basketball practice. Got to take her to it. Cheryl's working a double tonight. Got to be home with the kids. Can't.

> (**REGGIE** *leaves – disgruntled.* **FAYE** *watches after him with concern. Turns and looks at* **DEZ**.)

FAYE. You gon' get enough of sickin' at his heels.

DEZ. Lucky I ain't bite.

FAYE. Need to back off of him. Like to push people too far. He been a good supervisor to us. You know that.

DEZ. He holdin' somethin' back and I think you know it too.

FAYE. What's it matter whether or not he tells you what you wanna hear? Until word comes from HR, we ain't got much to stand on.

DEZ. You the rep. You supposed to be on our side. Fighting for us. What happened to all that union talk you got every other day? That only apply to everybody but Reggie?

FAYE. Oh I see, you in a fightin' mood today. Now you wanna throw punches with me? Hunh? You take yo' best shot.

DEZ. Ain't nobody tryin' to fight you.

FAYE. Naw. You feelin' froggy? Go'on and leap!

DEZ. Fine then. He ain't yo' son. That's what I got to say.

FAYE. Oh, now you just talkin' stupid.

DEZ. Am I? Then you tell me you don't got your blinders on when it come to him.

FAYE. I ain't got no blinders for nobody.

DEZ. Tell me why you ain't called no meetings down at the Local or demand this company let us know our fate. Tell me why we ain't talkin' health coverage or severance deals? Ain't even gonna prep us for the blow that might be comin'?

FAYE. You talkin' premature. Got to let the man do his job first. Let him rise to the occasion. If somethin's goin' down, he can help fight for our jobs. Can't define what a man is until he got to take an action. You judge him befo' we even see what the action gonna be. And me – what I know 'bout that man...what I knew 'bout his mama and what he's made of...when it come to where his heart lie, he gonna rise to the occasion.

DEZ. And if he don't?

FAYE. If if was a fifth, we'd all be drunk.

DEZ. You trust him so much...why you ain't tell him you livin' here?

FAYE. And we are now done with this conversation.

DEZ. So you can get in my ass but I can't in yours?

FAYE. You ain't got enough leverage to get in my ass. Besides, you talkin' 'bout somethin' you ain't got no proof about. You speculating and that's for lawyers and investigators, that ain't for you.

DEZ. Zero tolerance policy. That's what Reggie say. For all disorderly conduct. How disorderly you think it is to be livin' at the job?

FAYE. I don't abide by no rules but necessity. I do what I do 'til I figure out another thing and do that. And that's all I got to say about it.

DEZ. Fine.

FAYE. Now sit down and let me take yo' money.

(FAYE *pulls out a deck of cards. Shuffles them.*)

DEZ. I ain't supposed to be gamblin' no mo –

FAYE. Cut it.

(DEZ *reluctantly sits and cuts.* FAYE *deals.*)

This ain't a democracy. You in my personal breakroom and in the noble effort of thankin' me for not kickin' yo' ass out, you grant me the simple pleasures of playin' a game of cards so that I can graciously and repetitiously take yo' money. *(Shift.)* Crazy eights. Twenty-five to start.

(She puts cash on the table. DEZ *matches her.)*

DEZ. *(Dropping his first card.)* Hearts.

FAYE. You know, you ain't the only one in tough shit. When I first come up in this plant, I was pregnant with my first and only. Kinda like Shanita. My son's father ran off and I was assed out. Had dropped outta school to be with him so I ain't have no family to fall back on. My mama didn't play them kinda games – your move.

(She throws a card on the table. DEZ *plays.)*

She come from the real ol' school. Once you shame your mama and turn up with a fast tail, you got to be put out and ain't no lookin' back. I was scared shitless but somethin' in me knew I was gonna survive. Not cuz nothin' was promised to me or cuz I could see the light at the end of the tunnel or no shit like that. But somethin' in me knew what I was made of. I was gonna survive cuz I had to.

DEZ. On you.

(FAYE's turn.)

FAYE. So I walked up, hiding my pregnant belly so I could get me a job, and I got it. Same day. Been workin' the line ever since. Survivin' ever since – take two.

DEZ. Awwwww...

(DEZ takes two cards.)

FAYE. And it ain't been no easy work all the time. Even got the battle scars to prove that stamping doors ain't for sissies.

(FAYE holds up her arm for DEZ to see. A scar skates along her forearm.)

This beauty right here...from a press machine on twelve-line. Years ago. Got backed up and tried to pull the sheet metal that was stuck in the gears. Press came right down by my hand, sparks burned the shit outta me. Coulda been a lot worse if I ain't move my hand quick. That's fast thinkin' like you ain't never seen. But

I still got all my limbs. Everything in tact. Twenty-nine
years – knock.

DEZ. So that's the lesson? Faye's a survivor so shut the fuck
up and leave her alone? Spades.

(FAYE's *turn. She pulls cards.*)

FAYE. You know, you really stupid. I'm tellin' you about
being pregnant and alone. I'm telling you about
having a son and bein' clueless. I'm telling you about
not having the answers. Ain't never had 'em and
probably never will. But whatever I'm doin', it's keepin'
me here. And that's how I can be patient when the
plane is headed toward a tree, cuz even if it crash...I
don't think I'd die. I think I'd get scarred maybe. But
I wouldn't die. Take the train next time. Keep movin'
– Hearts.

DEZ. Well I'm tellin' you somethin' right now Faye.

FAYE. What you tellin' me?

DEZ. If the plane is crashing, I ain't gonna sit and watch it
go into a tree. I'm goin' in that cockpit and I'm takin'
the pilot's life jacket. I'm takin' the pilot's parachute.
And I'm jumping from that motherfucker long before
it goes up in flames. You can tell that to Reggie or
whoever the hell needs to know. I'm gettin' what's
mine...

(FAYE *glares at* DEZ.)

(FAYE *pulls a card.* DEZ *pulls and throws one.*
FAYE *pulls again. Her hand is getting full.*)

FAYE. It's gonna come with a price. Just like that scar you
got behind your ear.

(DEZ *stops playing for a moment. Touches his scar.
Strangely self-conscious. Then he releases. Goes
back to the cards.*)

(DEZ *gains speed. Down to only a few cards.* FAYE
has a full hand.)

FAYE. You can pretend you and me ain't affected by the same things, except we both got battle scars. But your way is impatient. May work for you in the short-term. But in the long-term, it kills.

DEZ. It's what I am Faye.

FAYE. A hot head?

DEZ. A warrior. See?

>*(He drops his last card.)*

Game.

FAYE. Fuck!

>*(FAYE slams her hands down on the table. DEZ scoops the cash.)*

One more.

DEZ. Naw naw...can't. If Reggie catch me, he's gonna throw me to the wolves. That was my last game on the premises.

FAYE. He's just scaring you cuz you piss him off.

DEZ. Whatever. I ain't takin' that chance. Need me a good severance deal...*if*...shit goes down.

FAYE. If if was a splif, we'd all be high.

>*(DEZ rises from the table. Goes to his locker and grabs his goggles, puts on his sweatshirt, etc.)*

>*(SHANITA enters. Tears in her eyes. Visibly upset.)*

Shanita, come let me take yo' money.

>*(FAYE stops when she sees SHANITA – who ignores both FAYE and DEZ. Goes to her locker.)*

DEZ. What's the matter with you?

FAYE. You alright?

>*(SHANITA doesn't answer. Her head in her locker. She bites back a wail. Beat.)*

>*(She grabs her goggles. Closes locker.)*

>*(Then she moves past FAYE, and exits.)*

>*(They both look after her with concern.)*

DEZ. See that? Some people head right into that tree, crash, and don't survive. You gotta think about them, too...

> (DEZ *grabs his goggles and exits.*)
>
> (FAYE *alone – shuffles cards. And shuffles cards. And shuffles cards.*)

Scene Four

*(SHANITA in the breakroom. Early morning. Sips
a cup of coffee. Silence. FAYE enters, half-dressed.
Putting on her work clothes. SHANITA says
nothing. Reads a book of names.)*

FAYE. That coffee good today?

SHANITA. It's alright.

FAYE. I tried to make it like before. Don't think I mixed it
the same.

SHANITA. It's alright.

*(FAYE walks past the bulletin board. Sees the sign
"CRIME ALERT." Shakes her head.)*

FAYE. You hear about the plant gettin' ripped off again?

SHANITA. Again?

FAYE. Say this morning on nine-line, more materials were
missing. Don't even know how they got off with it.

SHANITA. Everybody on three-line say they been installing
more cameras on the floor. Heard they just hired a
night watchman to patrol the grounds after dark.

(A quick beat.)

FAYE. That right? *(Pause.)* Where he gonna be stationed?

SHANITA. Don't know. Just say they increasing security
everywhere.

(FAYE registers this. Shift.)

FAYE. How that little honey bun you got cookin' in the
oven? Started kicking yet?

SHANITA. Only sometimes. At night mostly.

FAYE. Started having cravings yet?

SHANITA. Not really. Tryin' not to eat a lot so I don't get
fat. Gotta keep the weight off.

FAYE. Keep the weight off? If it's one time a woman
supposed to feel like enjoying the full pleasures of
eatin', it's when she's with child. Somebody done put

that in yo' head? Got yo' mind on weight when it's 'spose to be on tendin' to your child's needs.

SHANITA. That's easy for you to say Faye.

FAYE. How's it any easier for me than for you?

SHANITA. Woman with kids already got a uphill battle. It put a mark on you that keep everybody away.

FAYE. Like I say, how you figure it's easier for me?

SHANITA. Cuz you off men. That make it different, don't it?

FAYE. You think it's easier cuz I like women? Think heartbreak only come in opposites?

SHANITA. I ain't never known a woman to make me feel all the ways men make me feel. Crazy and so upset I can't breathe sometimes.

FAYE. Love ain't never had no kind of particulars, far as I'm concerned. Love just whatever it show up as. But love don't send you into the breakroom in tears every three days.

SHANITA. Don't talk about it Faye.

FAYE. I ain't gonna talk about nothin'.

(Beat. SHANITA changes the subject.)

SHANITA. Make you dream crazier though. Bein' pregnant.

FAYE. Oh yeah?

SHANITA. My Big Mama used to say dreams from a pregnant woman actually more like prophecies. You ever heard that?

FAYE. Sound like somethin' a Big Mama would say.

SHANITA. I don't know if it's any truth to it or whatever. But I been having these same dreams over and over. I'm standing on a concrete floor. Big empty space with nothin' in it. Dust covering everything. I call out the names of people. Y'all mostly. But nobody answer. Then comes a strong gust of wind. When it stop, the dust is scrambled in a group of letters that don't spell nothin'. Crazy, right?

FAYE. I'll say.

SHANITA. I think it could be a sign. From my baby maybe. Like whenever I can unscramble the message, everything's just gonna be clear.

FAYE. Everything like what?

SHANITA. I dunno. Life. *(Quick beat.)* You think that's silly?

FAYE. Maybe so. But don't mean it ain't also possible.

(Quick shift.)

SHANITA. Where Dez?

FAYE. Think he must be runnin' late today.

SHANITA. Didn't walk me to my car yesterday. Guess he busy.

FAYE. If he don't punch in in the next five minutes, he gonna have a write-up on his hands.

SHANITA. Cassie Logan down on my line got written up yesterday for leavin' two minutes before her break cuz she had to pee. Try to tell me I can't break when my baby pressin' down on my bladder. I don't think so.

FAYE. They crackin' down like that, huuh?

SHANITA. Some folk say it's just a scare tactic. Downsizin' and trying to weed out the people who slackin'. I decided I ain't gonna listen to all that hearsay. Cuz people gonna end up sabotaging themselves and get fired...and that ain't gonna be me. Plus, you our union rep. Everybody know you ain't gonna take no company shit.

(FAYE pauses. Concerned.)

FAYE. You got a plan for yourself, regardless?

SHANITA. Got offered a job over at the Copy Center on eight mile. My cousin used to be the manager, but she movin' offices. Said I could come take over.

FAYE. That sounds good.

SHANITA. Not to me. What I'm gonna do at a copy center? Day in and day out, runnin' paper through these simple machines – for what? Don't got the same kind of pride this work got. Here, I feel like I'm building somethin' important. Love the way the line needs me. Like if I step away for even a second and don't ask somebody to mind my post, the whole operation has to stop. My touch...my special care...it matter. I'm building something that you can see come to life at the end. Got a motor in it and it's gonna take somebody somewhere. Gonna maybe drive some important businessman to work. Gonna get some single mama to her son's football practice. Gonna take a family on they first trip to Cedar Point. Gonna even maybe be somebody's first time. Who knows? But I like knowing I had a hand in it, you know? That's why I'm gonna turn her down.

FAYE. Your cousin?

SHANITA. Don't wanna work at no copy center. What's life at a copy center?

FAYE. Maybe you don't wanna do that yet. Always nice to have somethin' behind you in case you need to cover yo' ass.

SHANITA. Cover my ass for what? Do somethin' I don't believe in? I figure ya'll is right. Time to stop worryin' about something that may not happen. Workin' in this industry is what I do. Uncertainty is always there. But it's the work I'm made of. In me from my daddy. Wanted a son, but got me instead. Always been good with my hands, and this somethin' that makes him proud of me. Not bein' pregnant before I'm married. Not being over twenty-five and building a family by myself. But this? Being a highly skilled job-setter...that's something I can stand on. Everybody can't say that. Everybody can't do what I do. I belong here. Ride it 'til the wheels fall off. Right?

(Pause. FAYE rises from the table.)

FAYE. I need a smoke.

SHANITA. Need to quit, Faye. Ain't good for you.

FAYE. Where my pack?

(SHANITA points to the counter. FAYE grabs her pack.)

SHANITA. You better do it outside. Don't wanna get caught breakin' the rules right now.

FAYE. I'll be back in a few. See you out on the floor.

(FAYE *leaves.*)

(SHANITA *rises slowly. Goes over to the sink. Washes her dish.*)

(DEZ *enters hastily. Looking untidy.*)

DEZ. Reggie been in here yet?

SHANITA. Not yet. You got like thirty seconds to punch in.

(DEZ *rushes to the clock. Punches in his card.* SHANITA *turns to look at him.*)

What happened to you?

DEZ. Nothin'.

SHANITA. Something.

DEZ. Got into a fight.

SHANITA. With who?

DEZ. Some fools on Gratiot *[Pronounced: Gra-shit, like "Mash-it"].* Stopped at the gas station and them niggas tried to rob me.

SHANITA. You for real? This morning?

DEZ. Yeah.

SHANITA. What happened? You alright?

DEZ. Yeah I'm alright. Tried to jump me. We got into it for a sec but I got out of it.

SHANITA. How?

DEZ. I just did.

(DEZ *goes to make some coffee.*)

SHANITA. What happened to you yesterday?

DEZ. Yesterday when?

SHANITA. After work. The parking lot? You wasn't there.

DEZ. Oh my bad. I had to run somewhere in a rush. Plus, I knew you was workin' late with Reggie. Figured he could walk you to yo' car if you needed somebody.

(Silence. **DEZ** *looks at* **SHANITA**. *Cracks a smile.)*

Why? You miss me?

SHANITA. *(A little.)* Boy please. I was just asking cuz you always make such a big deal of walkin' me, and then poof – you disappeared. Was just wonderin', that's all.

DEZ. Wondering for what?

SHANITA. Cuz you said you would. That's all. But obviously you're the kinda person that say they gonna do somethin' and then don't show up. Tell me everything I need to know.

DEZ. If I knew you cared, I'da shown up. To hell with my meeting.

SHANITA. Meeting?

DEZ. With some of my business partners. For my garage.

SHANITA. Meeting? Not a date?

DEZ. Which one make you more jealous?

SHANITA. Tccchhhh…neither.

DEZ. Neither?

> *(Pause.* **SHANITA** *and* **DEZ** *look at each other. A moment of possibility.* **SHANITA** *considers it for a moment…then quickly decides to shut it down.)*

SHANITA. *(As if answering her own question.)* You too reckless.

> *(***SHANITA** *heads out of the breakroom.)*

DEZ. I'll be there for you today. After work. Walk you to your car. If you want me to.

SHANITA. I won't be waiting.

> *(***SHANITA** *exits.)*
>
> *(***DEZ** *watches her go…his heart longing after…)*
>
> *(Then goes to his locker. Pulls an item from his locker. Wrapped in cloth. Peeks at the item, and breathes a sigh of relief.)*
>
> *(Finds a plastic bag nearby. Puts wrapped item in bag.)*

(Puts item back in locker. Closes and seals the lock. And heads out onto the floor.)

(As a spotlight closes in on the locker, silhouetted workers are illuminated...struggling to complete the stamping motion. More chinks in the rhythm. More dysfunction.)

Scene Five

(Morning on the breakroom. A bra hangs over the heater. The heater is on. Some panties are lying across the heater.)

(The boombox is on. A song by Aretha Franklin plays*.)

(FAYE enters in some pajamas. Maybe a makeshift robe. She goes through her morning ritual. We see her putting on deodorant. A towel over her hair from recent washing. She takes towel off. Begins to brush her hair into something presentable. Eats some toast.)

(FAYE checks the panties on the heater. Feels that they are dry. Slides them on.)

(She pulls the bra off of the heater.)

FAYE. *(To the heater.)* Better not burn my titties.

(She continues to get dressed. Socks. Boots. Puts on lotion, etc.)

(At the breakroom door: Someone attempts to enter. They can't get in. They knock.)

REGGIE. *(Offstage.)* Hello? Somebody in there?

(FAYE turns off the music. Quickly cleans up around her. Throwing things hastily into her locker. She fastens her bra. Squirms a bit from the dampness. Throws on a sweatshirt.)

(The beating at the door gets more rapid.)

---

* A license to produce *SKELETON CREW* does not include a performance license for music by Aretha Franklin. The publisher and author suggest that the licensee contact ASCAP or BMI to ascertain the music publisher and contact such music publisher to license or acquire permission for performance of a song by Aretha Franklin. If a license or permission is unattainable for the song, the licensee may not use a song by Aretha Franklin in *SKELETON CREW* but may create an original composition in a similar style. For further information, please see music use note on page 3.

(Offstage.) Whoever the hell is in there, you've got five seconds to open this door before I call the cops.

> (**FAYE** *grabs a cigarette. Lights it. Takes a few puffs.*)

> (*The doorknob shakes and shakes. Loud banging. The door rattles.*)

(Offstage.) One.

> (**FAYE** *takes another puff.*)

(Offstage.) Two.

> (**FAYE** *puffs.*)

(Offstage.) Three, gotdamnit.

> (**FAYE** *blows the smoke around the room. Fans it with her hands.*)

(Offstage.) Four asshole.

> (**FAYE** *puts out the cigarette. Grabs a room freshener and sprays.*)

(Offstage.) Alright. Be stupid then.

> (**FAYE** *opens the door. Sees* **REGGIE** *on his cell. He stares at her in disbelief for a moment and then hangs up.*)

FAYE. My bad.

REGGIE. Faye? What are you –?

> (**REGGIE** *enters the breakroom.*)

You've been smoking?

FAYE. You can tell? Damn.

REGGIE. The room reeks, Faye!

FAYE. I'm sorry.

REGGIE. You've got to stop this. Why didn't you say anything?

FAYE. Ain't wanna hear your mouth. Was just trying to cover it up.

REGGIE. Well you did a terrible job. It smells awful in here. How long were you – do you know what I was thinking?

FAYE. That I was one of those rip off artists?

REGGIE. Could've caused a big panic.

FAYE. And here you go – countin'.

REGGIE. I was trying to be fair.

FAYE. What were you gonna do if somebody opened this door ready to knock you silly? Count how many times they go upside your head?

REGGIE. You know I was about to call the cops on you?

FAYE. I figured I had 'til four and a half...four and three quarters...

REGGIE. *(Laughs faintly.)* That's not funny.

FAYE. Yes it is. I'm sorry. I just needed me an early smoke and it's too damn cold this morn to do it outside. *(Shift.)* They figured out who's been stealing that stuff anyway?

REGGIE. Not yet. Upstairs is cracking down on all of us.

FAYE. So what's that mean?

REGGIE. That means I'm going to be doing some investigating. I need you to report anything out-of-the-ordinary to me. Everybody, for that matter. I want to make sure they know our unit is part of the solution and not the problem. Whole management team has a lot of pressure on us not to let this thing get any more out of control.

FAYE. Why's the pressure on you? How you supposed to stop it more than anybody else?

REGGIE. It's happening on one of our shifts. Somebody's got to be responsible.

> *(Pause. REGGIE takes down signs from the bulletin boards. Posts new ones.)*
>
> *("Fridge Emptied Every Friday.")*
>
> *("You See Your Mama Here? No? Then Clean Up After YOURSELF!")*
>
> *("Stop And Search Policy In Effect.")*
>
> *(FAYE's eyes bore through REGGIE.)*

FAYE. You got a sign in there from HR?

REGGIE. Not yet, Faye.

FAYE. What about fighting to keep this place open? Shifting the production schedule to keep us working?

REGGIE. I brought that up. Harris says he'll give it some thought.

FAYE. Draggin' ya heels, ain't you?

REGGIE. …

　　…

　　…

There's a lot going on right now. This theft is throwing a monkey wrench and this production schedule is a tall task and –

FAYE. *(Like a dagger.)* Excuses.

　　(Tense beat.)

People need notice.

REGGIE. I'm pushing for that.

FAYE. Health care. Survival money.

REGGIE. You think I don't know that?

FAYE. This could sink some of us. Be the nail in our coffin. Folks got kids to provide for. Contracts demand we get a fair notice.

REGGIE. You bringing up contracts, Faye? You think I'm not doing my part?

FAYE. Tuition reimbursement. Re-training support. Cobra plans that don't kill us. You got a good relationship with Harris. Time to make it count.

REGGIE. You don't think I'm pulling his coat to all that? You think this is me?

FAYE. Ain't sayin' it's you.

REGGIE. Early panic, Faye. The company is afraid of it. Thinks it will impact production for the rest of the year.

FAYE. Is that what you think?

REGGIE. Doesn't matter what I think.

FAYE. It matters.

(Beat.)

REGGIE. Faye, I'm a good foreman.

FAYE. I know you are.

REGGIE. I'm not the enemy.

FAYE. I didn't say you were.

REGGIE. Then don't question me. Please. I'm doing everything I can.

(REGGIE continues with his signs.)

FAYE. Shanita got a job offer.

REGGIE. She did? Where?

FAYE. Copy Center. Eight-mile. Can run it herself and probably earn a decent wage for her and her little one.

REGGIE. *(To himself.)* Huh…

FAYE. She's gonna turn it down Reggie.

REGGIE. She say that?

FAYE. Verbatim.

(Pause. REGGIE contemplates.)

REGGIE. I can talk to Harris. See if we can get her placed somewhere else.

FAYE. Without seniority? She got a definite. You want her to wait on a maybe?

REGGIE. Her record is impeccable. I know we can get her re-situated somewhere.

FAYE. Just like you?

REGGIE. That's right. Just like me. That's what I'm working on. That's the line I have to walk, Faye.

FAYE. You think about what walking that line is costing everybody else?

REGGIE. Of course I'm thinking about it! I don't like it. But what else can I do? I don't own this place, I just try to keep it running smoothly.

FAYE. I been holding off for you Reggie. Was a time when I'd grab these folk and take to the damn street. Shut this place down until they do right. To hell with

company interests. You got the ear of your supervisor.
That's a rare spot to be in. You tell Harris it's time to be
transparent. Production'll just have to be what it'll be.

REGGIE. He's not going to listen to all of that, Faye!

FAYE. What is he going to listen to? You thought about
that?

REGGIE. I'm thinking about that! I'm also thinking that I
need my job just like everybody else. If this company
folds, I could fold with it. I don't have a union to protect
me. I just have my reputation. A rep that could get me
placed somewhere else. Ohio maybe. Out in Virgina
would be nice. If I start rousing things up before it's
time, I'm gonna be the one to lose out. My kids. My
wife. I'm thinking about Shanita. I'm thinking about
Dez. I'm thinking about you. Bony J. I'm thinking about
Elder Johnson who's been working the line for forty-
five years. The man's been in my house. Buys Christmas
presents for my kids. And I'm thinking on what'll
happen to him if he doesn't get the right package. I'm
thinking about Dalina and Darnell...how much they
love bringing friends over to the house now. How often
they hang outside because they feel safe. How I could
lose my job and make my family lose everything we've
been – I'm walking the line, Faye. One foot in front of
the other and trying not to fall and crash and break my
spine. And who am I going to lift up when I'm broken?
How can I help anyone else if I don't help myself? I'm
thinking about it, Faye. I'm thinking about Shanita.
I'm thinking about Dez. I'm thinking about you. I'm
thinking and I'm thinking and I'm thinking – okay?!

FAYE. Okay.

   (Air.)

Sound like your mama right now.

REGGIE. How's that?

FAYE. Just how she would say "shut up Faye" or "back off
Faye" without really sayin' nothin' at all.

REGGIE. I wouldn't tell you to shut up.

FAYE. No. You got too much sense to do that. But you tellin' me somethin' alright.

(*Beat.*)

REGGIE. Cheryl's been asking about you. Said to tell you she misses your peach cobbler.

FAYE. Yeah well...maybe I'll stop by one of these weekends and take over your kitchen.

REGGIE. Or we come to you. Whatever's easier.

FAYE. I come to you.

REGGIE. The kids'll be happy to see you.

FAYE. Sho.

REGGIE. I got to get on upstairs, Faye.

FAYE. Yeah.

(**REGGIE** *heads to the door.*)

I know you thinkin', Reggie. But you come to a conclusion real soon, you hear me? Otherwise, I'm gonna come to one first. Cuz I can't let these folk fall with nothin' to stand on. Secret or no secret. Family or not. You understand that?

(**REGGIE** *looks at* **FAYE**, *almost incredulous.*)

REGGIE. What are you saying?

FAYE. Think fast.

(**REGGIE**, *concerned...exits.*)

Scene Six

*(Nighttime falls on the breakroom. It is empty.
Sounds at the door.)*

REGGIE.	DEZ.
(Offstage.) I need to get in there and there's not a damn thing you're going to do to stop me. You don't like to listen. You never like to follow any damn rules. Get out of my way, Dez. I swear to God you better get out of my way.	*(Offstage.)* What the hell you tryin' to go through my stuff for, hunh? I ain't see no warrant. You wanna go through my shit, you gotta get somethin' or else you gonna have to walk through me. I ain't movin' nowhere.

(DEZ opens the door with REGGIE at his heels.)

DEZ. I swear to God, you need a warrant.

REGGIE. I don't need a warrant while we're on work grounds. This isn't your personal house, Dez. That's what you don't understand.

DEZ. You don't know what I understand.

REGGIE. I'm going to ask you one more time Dez. Open your bag, or else I'm getting the clippers and we're cutting this lock.

DEZ. What the hell am I? A criminal?

REGGIE. Better not be.

DEZ. Why you gotta act like such a bitch, man?!

REGGIE. Watch your gotdamn mouth, Dez!

(FAYE and SHANITA enter the breakroom hastily.)

FAYE. What's going on in here?

SHANITA. Can hear ya'll all the way down the hall.

DEZ. This nigga wanna test me –

REGGIE. I'm not yo' nigga –

DEZ. – Cuz I didn't want him going through my bag.

REGGIE. Because you're being insubordinate.

FAYE. Why're you going through his bag?

REGGIE. Do you all even read any of the signs I post? Mandatory stop and search. Employees are asked to empty their bags when exiting the building –

DEZ. At random –

REGGIE. It happens to everyone.

DEZ. And today it only happened to happen to me.

REGGIE. It was a random search, Dez. We've been hit a lot lately. It's perfectly fair.

DEZ. Fair to who?

REGGIE. Fair to everyone! I put up a notice. It wasn't out of the blue. You act like it was out of the blue.

SHANITA. I got stopped yesterday. Just opened my bag and showed 'em it wasn't full of nothin' but pre-natal pills. No big deal. They let me out and I went home.

DEZ. That ain't what this is about.

REGGIE. What is it about then Dez, hunh?

DEZ. You know what this is about Faye.

FAYE. Faye? How'd I get into this?

DEZ. Cuz you always protecting this dude –

FAYE. Don't bring no Faye into this.

(The sound of radio static interrupts.)

VOICE THROUGH STATIC. Status Report. All units in?

(REGGIE grabs the radio on his hip.)

REGGIE. *(To radio.)* Handling a dilemma. Status update in two minutes. *(Shift.)* Dez, stop stalling. I've got to report back. Get past your foolish pride and open your bag. Or I'm going in the locker. It's that simple.

DEZ. I ain't opening shit.

SHANITA. Dez just open the bag!

DEZ. Ain't right.

FAYE. *(To REGGIE.)* What you need to know about him? Tell me and I'll school you. Been watching him come and go every damn day.

REGGIE. It's simple protocol. I look in Dez's bag. He's cleared and goes home. It doesn't have to be this difficult. He's making it difficult.

DEZ. I ain't making shit difficult –

REGGIE. Unless he has something to hide.

DEZ. You accusing me of something?

REGGIE. I'm not accusing, I'm inquiring –

FAYE. Dez ain't stealin' nothin'. He's a fool but he ain't that stupid.

REGGIE. If I don't search him, the cops will. He can make this a lot easier.

DEZ. To hell with you and the cops.

REGGIE. Dammit Dez! I'm going to ask you one more time –

SHANITA. Dez just do it!

DEZ. Do what?! Prove something? Won't matter! Once you got your mind made up about me you got your mind made up. What I'm supposed to do? Change it? Convince you I'm not the shit that you done convinced yourself I am? That's supposed to be my burden? My job? Hunh? Fuck that. Nigga always on me about somethin' –

REGGIE. You break the rules!

DEZ. Always treating me like I'm up to no good. Like I ain't got a righteous bone in my body. Won't matter why I do what I do or what my intentions are. Won't matter what plans I got or what I'm trying to build. You got your mind made up that I'm shit and you just waiting for proof. So open the locker, then. Get your gotdamn proof. But don't ask me to volunteer for this bullshit. Just do what you gotta do.

SHANITA. Dez.

REGGIE. Fine then.

> (**REGGIE** *picks up a pair of bolt cutters. He walks over to* **DEZ**'s *locker.* **FAYE** *looks at* **DEZ** *with concern. Then she walks over to* **REGGIE**.)

FAYE. You don't gotta humiliate him like this now. Ya'll both just over-heated. Step away, cool off and let me talk some reason into him.

REGGIE. I'm tired of being disrespected by him, Faye. I gave him a chance. He asked for this.

> (REGGIE *reluctantly clips the lock. He opens the locker. Pulls out a pair of goggles. Some boots. Gym socks. Other personal items. Deodorant, cologne, a brush, etc.*)

> (DEZ *stands defiant.* REGGIE *finds nothing significant. He approaches* DEZ.)

The bag.

> (DEZ *doesn't move.*)

DEZ. (*Sucking teeth in defiance.*) Tttttchhh...

REGGIE. The bag. Or we call the cops.

> (DEZ *stands defiant.* SHANITA *and* FAYE *look on with concern.*)

> (REGGIE *reaches for* DEZ's *bag.* DEZ *doesn't protest. He doesn't resist. He remains stoic.*)

> (REGGIE *opens* DEZ's *bag. Pulls out the gun.*)

> (SHANITA *quietly gasps with concern.*)

What –

> (REGGIE *sighs with disappointment. Pulls out a plastic bag. Peers inside. Sees the wrapped material.*)

> (*Holds it out to* DEZ.)

Bullshit, hunh?

> (*The radio on* REGGIE's *hip goes off. The sound of static.*)

VOICE THROUGH STATIC. Unit nine, status update? ...Unit nine, status update?

(DEZ is silent. REGGIE puts the material back into the bookbag. Puts the gun back inside. Holds the bag.)

(All eyes on REGGIE, waiting breathlessly for his reply.)

(REGGIE looks at DEZ. At everyone. Sets the bag back by DEZ' foot. And exits.)

End of Act One

ACT TWO

Scene One

(DEZ, SHANITA, and FAYE in the breakroom. A few minutes have passed. FAYE sits across from DEZ. DEZ still has his coat on. He is a wall. SHANITA tries to fill the silent space.)

SHANITA. *(Nervous chatter.)* This whole city is under construction. That's what I discovered on my way into work today. Traffic on the 75 was crazy. They done took everything down to one lane. And people don't know how to merge. Cars backed up for miles cuz people don't know how to merge. Don't matter what freeway you take, it be the same selfish behavior on all of 'em. Everybody got somewhere to be and don't wanna let you in. Even when you honk at 'em. Even when you try to smile pretty and be polite with it. That shit used to work at one point. I could always squeeze into a lane with a smile. But not no more. Nobody wants to merge no more. We just gettin' squished into smaller lanes while they make these promises to fix the freeways and don't seem like they ever really get fixed. And at the end of the day, we just hate drivin' with each other cuz ain't enough space and assholes don't wanna let you in. And all I can think anymore is if we just merged, shit would flow so much better.

(FAYE sets a cup of coffee in front of DEZ.)

DEZ. No thanks.
FAYE. Drink.
DEZ. Not thirsty.
FAYE. Drink.

(DEZ grimaces at FAYE. Then takes the coffee and sips. SHANITA remains lost in thought.)

SHANITA. And I think I'm getting road rage. A big Mack Truck ran me onto the shoulder of the freeway last week. I got so angry, I grabbed my chocolate Frosty from Wendy's and threw it at his window.

But it just kinda sailed in the air and burst in the middle of the street. It was pretty anti-climactic. *(Beat.)* Damn road rage. Damn construction. Maybe we just need a whole new city.

FAYE. You better take a yoga class and calm yo' ass down. Don't wanna throw your Frosty at the wrong car.

SHANITA. I need to quit Frosties anyway 'fore I get fatter than I already am.

FAYE. Don't start that talk again.

SHANITA. I been doing good except for those. And also brownies.

(She breaks a piece of brownie and slides it over to DEZ. He sits stoic.)

DEZ. I'm good.

SHANITA. Eat it.

DEZ. Ain't hungry.

SHANITA. Don't matter.

(DEZ looks at SHANITA. She's not playing.)

(DEZ bites into the brownie unenthusiastically.)

(They watch him eat. Silence.)

What you think Reggie tellin' 'em?

FAYE. Ain't sure.

(Pause.)

SHANITA. He don't seem like he would snitch. Think he would snitch?

FAYE. Reggie got a lot to deal with.

DEZ. Here she go.

FAYE. Don't start turnin' on me now. I done fed yo' ass some coffee.

DEZ. Ain't startin' nothin' with you.

SHANITA. Why you bringin' that gun up in here, Dez?

DEZ. Same reason you throwin' Frosties at Mack Trucks.

SHANITA. Oh – so you pregnant and hormonal too?

DEZ. Shit gets personal on the street.

SHANITA. This ain't the street.

FAYE. You gon' tell us what that was Reggie found in yo' bag? Or you just want us all to pretend we ain't see that?

DEZ. What I got to answer to you for?

FAYE. Ain't said you had to answer to me.

DEZ. Tired of bein' questioned.

FAYE. Maybe if you gave some answers folks wouldn't have so many damn questions about you.

DEZ. Maybe I don't need everybody in my business all the damn time. Ain't asked you for your help. And you ain't one to talk about answerin' folks. You the last person to point that finger.

FAYE. You ain't me Dez. When you gonna learn that?

DEZ. You slide around here under the radar and defend everything that dude do, and don't even got the decency to let us know the plant closing.

SHANITA. That's just a rumor.

DEZ. Ain't no rumor. That's a fact. And Faye know it too. Closing this year, ain't that right Faye?

FAYE. Dez, stop talking stupid. You gon' cause Shanita unnecessary stress.

SHANITA. Folks always talk about the plant closing. Always threats.

DEZ. 'Cept these ain't just threats. Management droppin' down every department. Keepin' on just enough people to get the job done. Anybody ain't crucial to the line gettin' cut. Ain't that right, Faye?

SHANITA. Faye what's he talkin' bout?

(Pause. FAYE *glares at* DEZ.)

FAYE. This how you wanna do this? Really?

DEZ. I could ask you the same thing.

SHANITA. Rumors true?

*(*FAYE *looks at* SHANITA *for a moment.)*

FAYE. It ain't that I wasn't planning on sayin' nothin'. That ain't it. I was just handling things internally first.

SHANITA. We getting shut down, Faye?

FAYE. I ain't got no thorough report yet. Been working on getting as much info as I can.

DEZ. Info from Reggie, ain't that right? He told you somethin'. And 'fore we get dropped, you could be organizing with UAW to make sure we get took care of right, 'steada sittin' back protecting Reggie.

FAYE. Ain't nobody been sittin' back on nothin'. I been drawing out terms while Reggie works with management on –

DEZ. Work with management?! Since when is that how we negotiate?

SHANITA. Faye, what's gonna happen to us? We gonna lose everything?

FAYE. I ain't gonna let that happen to you.

DEZ. You done already proved where your loyalty be. Ain't with us.

SHANITA. I can't believe this. You wasn't gonna tell us Faye?

FAYE. 'Course I was gonna tell you! You think I ain't been stressin' over this every night? Shit, I done had plenty of stresses and this plant closing is only one of 'em.

DEZ. We all got stresses but I think you got yo' blinders on for somebody ain't deservin' –

FAYE. What you know about deserving?!

DEZ. I know Reggie ain't on our side. I know he get set up right he be taken care of. Everybody just out to protect themselves – keep they own neck from gettin' broke.

Don't matter how many other necks get snapped down
below, as long as your family took care of.

FAYE. That's your problem. You only know how to see shit
through small cracks and not the whole damn picture.
You think he ain't got nothin' to lose? You think you
the only one in limbo when this place shut down?

DEZ. Faye, what's the reason when it come to Reggie you
can't see a spade for a spade? The rest of us see it and
you still callin' hearts. That nigga ain't no heart. He's
a spade.

FAYE. You blame Reggie for everything this plant do to
keep you in line, but Reggie ain't make you bring that
gun up in here. That was you. That wasn't nothin' but
you.

SHANITA. Did you take them materials Dez?

DEZ. What if I did, hunh? What difference will it make?

SHANITA. Makes a lotta difference. Makes you a thief.

FAYE. Thief and a liar.

DEZ. A liar? That's supposed to mean somethin' coming
from you?

FAYE. I ain't took nothin' from nobody. That's a low I ain't
never sunk to.

DEZ. Ya'll gotta be kiddin' gettin' moral on me right
now. You think any of this is moral? Keep us workin'
these presses 'til we pull a fuckin' shoulder blade,
and then replace us in a heartbeat if we can't keep
up the production. You think when this ship sinks the
captain's going down? Ya'll got this blind faith in a crew
that don't even eat lunch with you. Don't know your
kid's first name.

FAYE. What's my son's name, Dez?

DEZ. That ain't the point.

FAYE. What's his name?

DEZ. You the one don't never talk about him.

SHANITA. What is your son's name?

FAYE. I rest my case.

DEZ. What case is you trying to make?

FAYE. Your whole philosophy is bullshit. You stealin' from the plant, don't try to make it nothin' righteous. Don't try to make it a cause. You want to be a thief? Be a thief. But don't try to hustle us into believing this is some sort of way to seek justice. You work. You sweat. You fight to have somethin' fair and right for yourself before you die. That's the industry. That's what we signed up for.

SHANITA. That ain't what I sign up for. A crapshoot. I signed up for a future.

FAYE. And you still gonna have one. You got a lotta potential to get placed somewhere else. Just keep doin' your best, and it's gonna mean somethin' for you. And Dez, if you ain't lose your cool, ain't no tellin' what you could build for yourself.

DEZ. Who say I'm not building? *(Beat.)* I got this homie that used to work down at WDZH before they moved stations. They started layin'off cats one by one 'til it was just this small crew left to cover the basics. Five dudes doing the work of twenty. And my boy was one of the five. They stayed on 'til the last two days when the station was getting stripped. Had all these materials that were going to be tossed to scraps, sold at auctions and whatever. Meanwhile, the homie had all these dreams of being a DJ. Was gonna start his own station. Here he was, sitting in the middle of tons of resources. Mixers. Turntables. Full DJ starter kit. Two days before his last day of work, they fired him. Said he wasn't working up to performance. Bullshit. And the homie left with nothing. No severance. No bonus. No studio of his own. Nothing. That was like three years ago. Just saw him working security down at the casino. Ain't even talkin' DJ'ing no more. And I remember him saying – "If I'd've known I was getting fired, I'd've robbed them blind." I remember that real clear. *(Beat.)* Don't assume we not building something. You don't even know.

FAYE. Did you take those materials Dez?

(DEZ and FAYE glare at each other.)

(A moment.)

(The door opens and **REGGIE** *enters. Everyone is silent. Waiting breathlessly for the decision.)*

REGGIE. Time for everybody to leave.

FAYE. What's going on?

SHANITA. Dez in trouble?

REGGIE. You need to get on outta here. All three of you.

SHANITA. What about – *(Seeing* **REGGIE** *'s tone.)* Alright...

DEZ. Fine by me.

*(***DEZ*** grabs his bag.* **REGGIE** *stands before him. They look at the bag.* **REGGIE** *finally moves out of* **DEZ***' path. Shaking his head.)*

REGGIE. You too, Faye. All of you need to go on home now.

*(***DEZ*** stops at the door. Looks at* **FAYE***.)*

FAYE. Okay. I'm right behind ya'll. Just gonna finish my pot of coffee. Ya'll go'on ahead.

REGGIE. Can't, Faye. Shift is over. I'm walking everybody out.

DEZ. I'll walk Faye out. Let her have her coffee.

REGGIE. You're in no position to give me orders. Get out of here Dez. Shanita. Faye. Everybody, let's walk.

*(***DEZ*** and* **FAYE** *look at each other knowingly.* **SHANITA** *heads to the door.* **FAYE** *carefully gathers her clothing. Slowly. Calculatingly. She finally puts on her coat and heads to the door.)*

(Her eyes bore through **REGGIE***. It's painful.)*

*(***DEZ*** is last. He and* **REGGIE** *look at each other. No words. Then finally:)*

DEZ. *(Shaking his head.)* Pssssshhhhhh...

REGGIE. ...

     ...

     ...

*(***REGGIE*** hits the light on the breakroom.)*

Scene Two

(Nighttime on the plant. The silhouetted workers on the line move slowly. Rigidly. The sounds of the plant create a slow and chilling mechanical orchestra.)

(Moonlight peeks through the basement-like windows on the breakroom.)

(Lights up on REGGIE, *looking around the breakroom. In his hands, a piece of* FAYE's *clothing.)*

(Suddenly a noise of someone fidgeting with the door. REGGIE *turns to look at it.)*

(The door opens and a hooded figure is revealed. The hood comes off and it's FAYE. *She stands to face* REGGIE.)*

(They stare at each other silently – in disbelief.)

REGGIE. Faye?

FAYE. ...

   ...

   Fuck.

(Uncomfortable silence.)

REGGIE. Faye. What are you – what the hell are you doing here?

FAYE. ...

   ...

   ...

REGGIE. You...haven't been...steal –

FAYE. No.

(More silence.)

REGGIE. Then what is this? Why are you here?

FAYE. What do you want me to say?

REGGIE. Whatever the truth is.

FAYE. The truth? Okay. *(Pause.)* It's cold as fuck out there tonight.

REGGIE. I don't understand.

FAYE. To sleep in my car, Reggie. It's too damn cold to sleep in my car. *(Beat.)* The truth.

REGGIE. Why're you sleeping in your...something wrong at home?

FAYE. Let's just leave it alone.

REGGIE. I can't leave it alone.

FAYE. Better if you don't know.

REGGIE. I'll be the judge of that.

FAYE. Just let it go, I said.

REGGIE. Faye, why can't you go home?

FAYE. Cuz I ain't got one. Satisfied?

REGGIE. What...happened to your house?

FAYE. I lost it, Reggie. Bank took it from me. That's all there is to it.

> *(Long beat.)*

REGGIE. ...

> ...

> ...

Why wouldn't you say anything? Why wouldn't you tell me?

FAYE. I ain't tryin' to hear no lectures right now. Just came to get warm.

REGGIE. How long have you been sleeping here?

FAYE. Long enough to piss you off.

REGGIE. Faye, goddamnit!

FAYE. 'Bout a month! Maybe longer.

REGGIE. A month?

> ...

> ...

FAYE. Thought it'd be better if you didn't know.

REGGIE. That's all you have to say?

FAYE. What you want me to say?

REGGIE. Say how! Why?

FAYE. I don't know what to tell you Reggie. Ain't nothin'
I can say that's gonna ease you none. I wasn't keepin'
up the payments on the note. Goddamn property
taxes killin' me. Roof was damn near cavin' in and I
couldn't afford to fix it up. Cancer treatments kickin'
my ass. What you want me to say? I ain't goin' through
my whole list of finances with you. Shit got out of my
hands. End of the damn story.

REGGIE. What about Jalen?

FAYE. You wanna know the last time I spoke to my son?
Let's see…well he got married 'bout three years ago.
Joined that new church on James Cousins. Had my
first grandchild some months later and told me he had
some concerns 'bout my lifestyle. Guessin' that pastor
done convinced him a lesbian grandmamma wasn't the
best influence or some shit.

REGGIE. Faye, I didn't kn –

FAYE. Fuck it. I see him on holidays. Ain't no tragedy. Just
is what it is.

(Silence.)

What you doin' here so late? You come to snoop on us?

REGGIE. I come here to think. Look for answers.

FAYE. Answers to what.

REGGIE. (Quick pause.) They want me to fire Dez, Faye.

FAYE. No.

REGGIE. Yes.

FAYE. They determined him the thief – just like that? No
hearin' or nothin'?

REGGIE. For his insubordination.

FAYE. What about the missing materials? The gun?

REGGIE. Didn't mention it. Tried to hold 'em off. Said I was
delayed cuz of his insubordination. So they say, we've
been needing to downsize. Why don't we release him.

FAYE. Dez a good worker.

REGGIE. I know it.

FAYE. Stubborn, but a good worker.

REGGIE. I know it Faye.

FAYE. Don't do it Reggie. Don't let 'em do it.

REGGIE. I'm trying – I just can't – *(Beat.)* You know what Cheryl told me the other day when I come home?

FAYE. What's that.

REGGIE. I look like I'm disappearing from myself.

FAYE. You got a lotta stress.

REGGIE. I'm tired of hearin' that.

FAYE. You ain't in a easy position.

REGGIE. I'm sick of walking that line.

FAYE. What line?

REGGIE. Line that say I'm over here and you over there and even though we started with the same dirt on our shoes...I'm supposed to pretend like you ain't more than an employee ID number. Like I don't know what happens out there when you leave these plant grounds. Why every man feels the need to arm himself before he walks into the grocery store or drops his kids off at school. Like I don't know the fear that's come over all of us lately. Walk around with your manhood on the line cuz you never know who's gonna try to take it from you. Cuz you never know when you're gonna be the next one out there, desperate and needin' to feed your family by any means necessary. I know Dez well, Faye. I look him in the eye and he scares the shit outta me. Cuz that invisible line between us...it's thin as hell.

FAYE. We all walk that line. Any moment any one of us could be the other. That's just the shit about life. One minute you passin' the woman on the freeway holdin' up the "will work for food" sign. Next minute, you sleepin' in your car, damn near...

(A moment. FAYE almost loses herself. REGGIE sees this.)

REGGIE. Faye what are we gonna do? You gotta tell me how to help.

FAYE. See this the shit I ain't want.

REGGIE. What d'you mean?

FAYE. Bein' made helpless. Strippin' me to the last scrap. Lose the house. The family. The job. Know what's left after that?

REGGIE. Faye –

FAYE. The soul. Then nothin'. I'm runnin' on soul now Reggie. Only thing still got fuel in it. And you and this pity…you gone run me to empty.

REGGIE. This ain't about pride, Faye.

FAYE. I grew up on the East side of Detroit, you know that? Seen buildings burn to the ground on Devil's Night. People squattin' in houses with no running water. My mama could barely afford to keep the gas on and we still found ways to stay warm. I don't like nobody questionin' my ability to rise up. I'm a born and raised East-sider. If it's one thing I know, it's how to rise the hell up.

REGGIE. How you gonna do that Faye? With no help? We supposed to be – I grew up at your house. My whole family – holidays. Barbecues. This don't just affect you, you know that? You keepin' this from me – it ain't right and it ain't fair!

FAYE. Don't tell me nothing about fair! It ain't fair it ain't fair – Life ain't fair! You think I don't know what I done? You think I'm some victim? I gamble goddamnit. Blow half my shit down at Greektown Casino. Now, you feel sorry for me? Started goin' down there twice a week. Then three times. You want me to tell you somethin' so it all make sense?

REGGIE. Yes I do –

FAYE. Your mama died.

REGGIE. …

FAYE. She was my heart and she gone and I couldn't move anymore without fuckin' somethin' up. I lose the people I give two shits about and I take it out on my pocketbook. Casino be the only place where nobody give a damn about you or your condition. They surround you with just enough strangers and noise that you feel halfway alright. And that was my choice. That's what I done. Now what about that? You still think that ain't fair? Or somewhere in your head, you figurin' I did this to myself?

REGGIE. I don't know what I think! *(Painfully.)* Dammit Faye…

> *(Long beat. Then a shift. He tries a new tactic.)*

We got a couch in the den. You come sleep there.

FAYE. Couch in here suit me just fine.

REGGIE. Faye, you can't…they'll find you. Tell me to let go of you next.

FAYE. I wish they would. Many years as I put in?

REGGIE. I don't know what's gonna come, Faye. You hear what I'm sayin'? I can't say it's gonna be good.

FAYE. I'm not asking you to make up happy endings. All I'm asking is that you tell 'em they can't write us off. We crucial to this production gettin' finished before they shut down. Tell 'em we need Dez. You got to fight for us, Reggie.

REGGIE. What about the materials?

FAYE. I don't think he stole nothin'.

REGGIE. You know that for a fact, Faye?

FAYE. I don't know nothin' for a fact. But I know Dez and he ain't no thief. You know it, too.

REGGIE. What the hell do I know? You living here right under my nose? How in the hell did I not – like I'm some distant –

FAYE. Reggie.

REGGIE. *(Urgently.)* Come home with me, Faye.

FAYE. ...

...

Let me stay for the night.

REGGIE. We can get you situated somewhere.

FAYE. Just give me time to think.

REGGIE. They put up cameras.

FAYE. Not in here. Patrolman ain't gon' bother me none.

REGGIE. What if they have footage of you?

FAYE. I move off-the-radar.

REGGIE. Faye, don't do this to me. I can't leave you like this.

FAYE. Reggie, I need you to let me be.

REGGIE. Faye –

FAYE. Just leave! *(Pause.)* Please. I need to do this. On my own.

REGGIE. ...

...

I...

> *(Silence. They look at each other for a moment.* **REGGIE** *is going to say more, but what's left to say?)*

If my mother knew I left you like this...

> **(REGGIE** *bites back his words. Walks out of the door. And disappears.)*

Scene Three

(Morning. The breakroom is empty. **SHANITA** *enters and digs in her bag. Pulls out a Tupperware dish and places it in the microwave.)*

*(***DEZ*** *enters with his things and looks at* **SHANITA**. *They are silent for a moment.)*

(The microwave buzzes. **SHANITA**'s *dish is ready. She goes to get it.)*

*(***DEZ*** *goes to his locker and puts up his belongings. As he places things inside, his bookbag falls to the ground.)*

*(***SHANITA*** *looks at it curiously. Says nothing.)*

DEZ. I ain't that stupid. Don't worry. Nothin' in here today. Not with folk invading my privacy.

SHANITA. I ain't said nothin'.

DEZ. I noticed. Not even good morning. Not even nothin' mean or rude. A brother can't even get a eye roll.

SHANITA. Ain't got nothin' to say.

DEZ. A'ight then…be that way.

(Pause. **SHANITA** *starts to eat her food. It is nothing skimpy or scarce like her usual. It's a full, hearty meal.)*

*(***DEZ*** *pulls out a pathetic sandwich from his bag. Maybe the bread is stuck together. He sits down next to* **SHANITA** *and picks at it pitifully. They eat silently.)*

SHANITA. Just stupid.

DEZ. You talkin' 'bout me?

SHANITA. Thinkin' aloud.

DEZ. Whatever.

(More silence. **DEZ** *picks apart his sandwich. It is falling apart. Gone from looking sad to looking diseased.* **SHANITA** *watches in disgust.)*

SHANITA. Gonna make me lose my breakfast watchin' you eat that.

DEZ. It's a perfectly good sandwich.

SHANITA. It look like roadkill. Just stop. Here.

> *(She grabs a nearby plate and puts some of her food on it. Slides the plate over to DEZ. He eats obediently.)*

DEZ. Damn girl! You put your foot in this. I ain't know you could cook like this.

SHANITA. I do alright.

DEZ. What you put in these potatoes? Got extra flavor.

SHANITA. Curry.

DEZ. That's what's up.

> *(More silence. A beat.)*

Thank you.

SHANITA. Whatever.

> *(Pause.)*

DEZ. Shanita...I –

SHANITA. Did you do it, Dez?

DEZ. I –

SHANITA. Did you steal them materials?

> *(DEZ looks at SHANITA in her eyes. Sincerity.)*

DEZ. No.

SHANITA. You swear?

DEZ. I swear. I ain't stole nothin'.

SHANITA. Then what was that Reggie found in your bag?

DEZ. Some brass fittings. Been collectin' 'em for my new shop. My boy held some for me from the Briggs plant. Had a auction. Went in there and got lots of stuff for my business. The fittings. Some weld caps. Even got me the hook-up on a clean engine for my car. That's all to it. I got 'em legit. Plant auction.

SHANITA. You swear?

DEZ. I swear. That's it. Only reason I even been bringin'
the stuff in is cuz I pick it up on my way into work.
Ain't gonna leave it in the car so niggas can break in
and steal the shit. These materials startin' to be like
gold over here. Take out a little at a time, it add up
eventually.

SHANITA. Why you ain't just tell Reggie?

DEZ. Reggie got in his head I'm shit.

SHANITA. But you coulda told him.

DEZ. So he can call me a liar? You know how exhausting
that is? To waste your time explaining yourself to
somebody who already got they mind made up about
you? No matter what I say, he gonna be hearin' it with
the screw face. Then after all that explainin', I done
wore myself out and he still gonna believe what he
gonna believe. I rather save myself the energy. Use it
toward something I give a damn about.

SHANITA. He believe you. We all believe you if you just say
so. You got it in your head that everybody your enemy,
even when they ain't. You thinkin' we just waiting for
you to prove us right. What we really doin' is holdin'
our breath to God that we wrong.

What we really doin' is wishin' on everything pure that
our fears don't come true. Don't nobody wanna see you
leave here defeated. Not none of us.

DEZ. Not you?

SHANITA. Not none of us.

(Beat.)

(Silence. DEZ looks at SHANITA.)

That gun. What you got to say about that?

DEZ. I can't say nothin' 'bout that.

SHANITA. Don't make no sense. It's like you sabotaging
yourself.

DEZ. I'm protecting myself.

SHANITA. From who?

DEZ. Everybody.

(Pause.)

SHANITA. I can't believe we getting shut down.

DEZ. We can all believe. Ain't the only ones. Been happenin' all over the city.

SHANITA. And still. Guess I just ain't wanna believe it could happen over here too. *(Beat.)* What we gonna do?

DEZ. You gonna be fine.

SHANITA. You don't know that for no fact.

DEZ. I do.

SHANITA. How you know?

DEZ. Cuz you good with yo' hands. You got skillz.

SHANITA. Boy stop tryin' to be slick.

DEZ. I ain't tryin' to be slick. I'm tellin' the truth. You one of the best out there – man or woman. Got like a talent in this or somethin'. You smart and you shine on the floor. That's not my opinion. That's a fact.

> (SHANITA *looks at* DEZ. *A moment of need. She grabs his face and kisses him spontaneously.)*
>
> *(It gets deep and passionate for a quick moment. Then she abruptly pulls away.)*
>
> (DEZ *is stunned.)*
>
> *(Pause. They look at each other.* SHANITA *moves away.)*

SHANITA. Shit. I'm sorry.

DEZ. Ummm…

SHANITA. I'm pregnant and my hormones are like shooting stars right now and I'm hungry and this is the first good meal I've had in like a month and I was tryin' not to get too fat and that was the nicest thing anybody's said to me in like a really fucking long time.

DEZ. Which…part…?

SHANITA. It can't be duplicated. Don't try.

> *(Beat.)*

I've been having these dreams lately. Crazy dreams.

DEZ. Like what?

SHANITA. Like this morning I dreamt I came into work like normal. Set my stuff up in the breakroom. Went on the floor and started work. And then I started gettin' these like awful contractions. And outta nowhere, I just start goin' into labor. Right on the shop floor.

DEZ. Aww shit. You better not. I ain't delivering no big-headed baby for you.

SHANITA. Shut-up Dez. My child will not be big-headed.

DEZ. I'm just sayin' though.

SHANITA. Anyway, I start pushin' and the baby wouldn't come out. And I'm pushin' like with all the might I got. And I'm sweatin'. And I'm over-worked. And I can see the dirt on my boots. And I'm pushin' and screamin' and the sound of the machines is screamin' with me... and soon as somethin' was 'bout to give...I just stopped. Contractions stopped. Feelin' of labor stopped. And the baby stay there in my belly...all this potential...still waitin' to be delivered.

DEZ. When the time comes, that baby's gonna take over the world.

SHANITA. You think so?

DEZ. It's a fact.

SHANITA. What you gonna do Dez?

DEZ. Try to stay on long as I can. Get my severance. Start my shop.

SHANITA. But what if they fire you?

DEZ. Then I just have to do somethin' else. That be the hustle.

SHANITA. You got quick answers for everything. You ever think anything all the way out?

(DEZ *is silent.*)

(*A moment of thought.*)

DEZ. All the time.

(*Beat.*)

(SHANITA *moves close to* DEZ.)

SHANITA. How you get that scar behind your ear?

DEZ. You got a million questions today.

SHANITA. Just answer it.

DEZ. Car accident. When I was a teenager. Headin' to the Cass vs. King football game with my boy Mike. Car rolled over on the shoulder of the 75. Flipped and landed right where I was sittin' on the passenger's side. Door near me got crushed and cut me along the back of my neck. Scar go down to the middle of my back. Folks had stopped along the side of the freeway and pulled me and my boy out. When the ambulance came, all I remember is folks sayin' how lucky we were to be alive. And I kept lookin' at that totaled car in disbelief. Wonderin' how I could survive somethin' so massive. And all them folks kept sayin' – if that car wasn't made good, we'd be dead. I remember that.

> (SHANITA *moves close upon* DEZ. *She touches his scar lightly.*)

SHANITA. I feel like nothing is familiar anymore. Everything just feel like right now. Like there's nowhere before this and nowhere after. You feel that?

DEZ. Sort of.

SHANITA. You know I ain't never broke a rule on-the-job in my life?

DEZ. I can believe that.

SHANITA. I'm gon' break one now.

> (SHANITA *kisses* DEZ. *Passionately. He receives it.*)
>
> (*They become increased in intensity. In need.*)
>
> (*They are embraced in passion. Clinging to one another for all they can...*)

Scene Four

(On the line: the silhouetted workers moving with precision. Then picking up speed. The stamping motion increases in rigor. Suddenly the workers are overworking – too many miles per hour. The overload is too much to bear. They begin to turn the motion onto each other. Fighting on the line. Attacking one another and going for blood. Lights crossfade from the chaos to the breakroom.)

(It's evening. FAYE *sits on the shabby couch and begins to unwind in her space.)*

(Suddenly REGGIE *bursts through the door – looking distressed. He closes the door urgently behind him.)*

REGGIE. I – I've done it.

FAYE. Reggie what you doin' down here? Thought your shift been over.

REGGIE. Was in a – in a meeting.

FAYE. I thought everybody done went home 'cept the guards and the nightshift. *(She sees* REGGIE*'s distress.)* What's the matter with you?

REGGIE. I can't – fuck me. Fuck fuck me!

FAYE. Reggie...

REGGIE. Faye I – I came down just to say – cuz I don't really know where else to –

FAYE. Reggie slow down, okay? You ain't...I can't follow you...Just slow down.

REGGIE. They pushed me Faye.

FAYE. Who pushed you?

REGGIE. It just all went too far, you know?

FAYE. What you talkin' about?

REGGIE. *(To himself.)* Goddamnit!

FAYE. What are you – *(Shift/resolve.)* They made you fire Dez.

REGGIE. No. I did it. I did what you said. I fought for him, Faye.

FAYE. Well that's good ain't it?

REGGIE. I told 'em he's too important. We need him on this crew. We need his skill to keep production moving on time. He's too valuable and we can't cut off our own hands to save our face. That's what I said.

FAYE. And what they say?

REGGIE. Said alright. Dez stays.

FAYE. Well good for you. That's a win.

REGGIE. Then Harris come talk to me private. Say...what about Faye Davison.

    (Quick pause.)

FAYE. What about me?

REGGIE. Say we oughta...

FAYE. *(Dangerously.)* What about me.

REGGIE. I don't even wanna – it was the way he said it that got in me wrong. It was the way.

FAYE. Said what.

REGGIE. Said to present you with the severance. Right now. Get you to retire.

FAYE. I just tell 'em no.

REGGIE. Say I oughta encourage it.

FAYE. Deal for twenty-nine years ain't the same as thirty.

REGGIE. I told 'im that.

FAYE. They can't make me retire. I know that much.

REGGIE. No but they can...they can make it real hard for you to stay. They can do that real good. And I did what you told me to do, Faye. I was ready to fight. I say no deal. Faye been at this company too long. She one of the most skilled workers we got.

FAYE. Been puttin' in shocks. Sewin' interiors. Stamping doors. Been all up through this work.

REGGIE. I told 'im that.

FAYE. And what he say?

(REGGIE's eyes shine with heartbreak.)

REGGIE. It was the way he said it that really made me – I just couldn't listen to him talkin' like that. Couldn't let him.

FAYE. What he say?

REGGIE. Spoke about you like you wasn't even – like you wasn't Faye. Like you had no name or no – history or no – "Dead weight" he say – just like that – like you wasn't even – I just couldn't let him. I felt it in my chest. Like dynamite burstin' inside of me.

FAYE. What you – what you meanin'?

REGGIE. I attacked him Faye.

FAYE. You did what?

REGGIE. I fuckin' – I – I attacked him. I attacked my supervisor.

FAYE. No.

(Long pause. Breathlessness.)

REGGIE. I'm – I'm done.

FAYE. No. *(Beat.)* WHY? – No. What'd you – how? How'd you attack him? You said somethin' to him?

REGGIE. *(Beat.)* Didn't say nothin' I just…I went for him. Just for a second. Like a shockwave went through me. Lunged at him like I was gonna pound him into the fuckin' ground. Like I was gonna grab him by the collar and crush that shit in my hands. Looked at him in his eyes. Seein' through that emptiness. That lack of feeling. That – whatever you call it – that make you stop seein' yourself in somebody else. And I flexed on him like – "Nigga I wish you would say some shit like that again. I will fuckin' kill you." 'Cept I ain't say it with words.

(Beat.)

Then the shockwave left me. Real fast. And I ain't touch him at all. Just got swole on 'im for a sec. But I came close enough. I would've. And he know it. And I know it too. I see him looking into my eyes like I'm the devil.

Can smell his fear. Like if he even breathes louder than a sigh I might kill him dead. And I might've Faye. I just might've.

(Beat.)

And I stand there, froze. Not knowin' if I really reached at him or if it was in my mind. But I see him lookin' at me – stiff. Like I scared the shit outta him. Like he was under attack. Like I'm *that* nigga. It's nothin' but silence between us for a sec. And then I just say, "NO DEAL." And I walk out.

FAYE. Reggie…

REGGIE. I'm done Faye.

FAYE. You ain't done. You ain't even touch him. You just gotta fix it.

REGGIE. Can't fix it. Ain't no way possible. I saw his fear. It's the little shit like that. Just a little bit of unraveling. That's all they need to mark me dangerous. I'm done.

FAYE. You got to try to fix it.

REGGIE. I can't! I can't fix none of this!

FAYE. Apologize to him.

REGGIE. I did what you said. I fought. I did exactly what you said Faye. You see that?

FAYE. I say fight! I ain't say sabotage yo'self!

REGGIE. You tell me how to do one without the other! You tell me how to fight and stand on some kinda ground in this industry without putting something massive on the line to do it! Ain't no way to fight without jumping on the goddamn grenade! Ain't no other way and you know it!

> (**REGGIE** *bangs his fist against the bulletin board.*
> *A sign falls. He begins tearing the rest of them*
> *down violently.*)

Goddamn lines. Goddamn rules. Goddamn everything!

> (*He falls against the wall and clings to sanity.*
> **FAYE** *watches him painfully. Silence.*)

(Long long beat. Then finally:)

FAYE. What if I took the deal?

REGGIE. What? I – No – What?

FAYE. What if you went back and told him Faye said she'll retire? Won't even cause no fuss.

REGGIE. No. You wouldn't get your – they'd cheat you. Rob you blind. And your health benefits wouldn't even – Wouldn't fix it no way Faye. I did what I did. I made myself a threat.

FAYE. But if you apologized. Went to Harris. Told him you got Faye Davison to walk. It'd show a effort, wouldn't it? It'd show cooperation.

REGGIE. Faye I can't –

FAYE. Yo' mama was so proud of you when you got this job. I won't ever forget the look on her face. Her son wearin' a button-up to work. Saw a different life for you than the one she knew. Life with a future. *(Beat.)* Me and her always joked that we wasn't never gonna be like none of these bums we seen on Woodward. Why be a bum in Detroit? Ain't make no sense, cold as it get. Soon as we get close to that last dime, we figure it make more sense to pay it on a bus ticket 'steada rent. Take us a trip down to Miami or Fort Lauderdale or somethin'. If we gon' be a bum, we'd say, might as well be a beach bum.

REGGIE. Faye...

FAYE. I could do that. Talk to Harris in the mornin' 'fore you even come in. By the time you get here? I already got my retirement deal and my one way ticket to somethin' else. Be like a ghost. A memory and nothin' more. And you stick around to fight another day.

(REGGIE looks at FAYE deliberately.)

REGGIE. I'm... *(Beat. Tears in his throat.)* I'm a man, Faye. I've done what I've done, and now I gotta go home. Gonna look my wife in the eye and tell her...cuz I've done what I've done. *(Beat.)* Tonight's your last night in this space, you hear me? Tomorrow, I come in here, clear out my desk, grab my belongings, and take you home with me. *(Pause.)* I'm taking you home.

> (**FAYE** *and* **REGGIE** *look at each other – a world of history and stories between them.*)

> (**FAYE** *reaches out to* **REGGIE**. *For the first time, they touch. She holds his hand. Squeezes it.*)

> (**REGGIE** *holds on firmly…*)

> (*Her grip the only thing keeping him from collapsing.*)

Scene Five

(Lights up on the breakroom. It looks different. Hard to determine why, but some things are not in place where they usually are. There is no deck of cards on the table. Some supplies may be missing from the shelves and the kitchenette. Perhaps stickers or pictures on a locker may be missing. Nothing completely obvious...but slightly emptier.)

(DEZ enters and heads to his locker. He takes off his coat and begins to prepare for work. He looks around the room, noticing that it feels strangely different. He cannot put his finger on it.)

(SHANITA enters. She heads over to her locker as well.)

(DEZ and SHANITA are strangely shy and awkward around each other.)

DEZ. Morning.

SHANITA. Morning.

(They go through their routine. SHANITA takes in the strangeness of the space. Unsure of what's different. She heads over to the coffeemaker.)

Nobody made coffee yet?

DEZ. Guess not.

SHANITA. Faye must not be in yet.

DEZ. Hm. Yeah... *(DEZ looks around for FAYE's things.)* Must not...

SHANITA. I'll make some.

(SHANITA goes to the shelf. A load of coffee sits in the basket. A note on them. She pulls it.)

Ohh...the good coffee! She got some more! *(Reads the note.)* "Shanita and Dez – That good shit. Faye." – That's so sweet! I gotta make sure to thank her when she get in.

*(DEZ looks around curiously. SHANITA eagerly
puts the coffee in the maker. Finally it dawns on
DEZ.)*

DEZ. The signs!

SHANITA. What's that?

DEZ. That's what's missing.

(SHANITA looks at the board.)

SHANITA. Ohhhh – shit you right! I knew it was somethin'.
Couldn't put my finger on it.

DEZ. That's gon' send Reggie through the roof.

SHANITA. Think it was whoever broke in?

DEZ. Maybe.

SHANITA. On my way in this morning that's all anybody was
talkin' about. Say somebody jammed up the sixteen-
line real good. Took some material off it too.

DEZ. Sixteen-line? That's a mutha. Whoever did that ain't
fuckin' around. They went straight for the biggest line
up in here.

SHANITA. I know. Wonder what it'll mean. *(Pause.)* Reggie
tell you what they decided about your, um –?

DEZ. Guess I'm gonna find out when I see 'im.

SHANITA. Cool…

*(The coffee maker runs. The refrigerator hums.
SHANITA sits and closes her eyes.)*

DEZ. Ay, so I was thinkin' maybe later if you wanna –

SHANITA. Shhhh…don't mess up the music.

DEZ. You still on that?

SHANITA. Just listen with me.

*(DEZ sits next to SHANITA. He watches her. She
keeps her eyes closed. DEZ looks at SHANITA. She
is glowing.)*

I used to fall asleep to all kinds of electronic music.
Sound of it come from the factory. Fills up the silence,
like it ain't never gonna disappear on you or let you go.

DEZ. You worry 'bout that a lot don't you?

SHANITA. What's that?

DEZ. People lettin' you go.

> (SHANITA *looks at* DEZ *and considers responding. She decides not to and instead closes her eyes again.*)
>
> (DEZ *eyes her hands on the table. She continues to listen. Slowly he reaches his hand out and delicately touches hers.*)
>
> (*Startled for a second, she opens her eyes and then closes them again quickly.*)
>
> (*They breathe together and listen to the sounds.*)
>
> (*The door to the breakroom opens. It's* REGGIE. SHANITA *snatches her hand away from* DEZ.)
>
> (*A look of urgent knowing on* REGGIE's *face.*)

REGGIE. Morning.

SHANITA. Morning Reggie.

> (REGGIE's *eyes dart around the breakroom toward* FAYE's *locker. Evidence of her presence is nowhere.*)

REGGIE. You all, um…there's a unit meeting today at three o'clock. You oughta both be there.

DEZ. Meeting for all staff?

REGGIE. That's right. For everybody who expects to stick around and learn the closing plan for the rest of the year. I'm gonna go through all of that.

SHANITA. You gonna talk us through post-closing too?

REGGIE. I am, Shanita. I'm going to make sure everything gets covered.

DEZ. So does that mean I should, um…

REGGIE. Means I'll see you at three o'clock Dez. That's what it means.

> (REGGIE *and* DEZ *stare at each other. The silence between them speaks volumes.*)

DEZ. Good then. I'll be there.

(SHANITA *breathes a sigh of relief. Beat.*)

SHANITA. Faye ain't in yet. You seen her on the floor?

REGGIE. No, she um...looks like she won't be coming back to work. I've just been informed that she's... (*With difficulty.*) retired early this morning.

DEZ. Retired?

SHANITA. Just like that? Without saying goodbye?

REGGIE. I think she um...felt that was best...

DEZ. That's crazy...

SHANITA. (*Softly.*) Damn...

> (*A moment. They settle into this new energy without* FAYE. *It feels strange.*)
>
> (REGGIE *regroups.*)

REGGIE. Be prepared for new safety updates at today's meeting. There was another robbery last night. Some of the brass fittings on sixteen-line have been removed.

SHANITA. They still don't know who it was?

REGGIE. No...this job was a little different. Doesn't look like the same person. Production on sixteen-line is shut down for the day. The sheet metal's been jammed and the backup sheets are missing from the warehouse. We need your skills on that line Dez. You're gonna be switched there for maintenance.

DEZ. Rippin' off the sixteen-line? That's some pro shit right there. Gotta be an inside job.

> (*Something dawns on* DEZ *immediately.*)

Yoooo!

SHANITA. (*Catching onto* DEZ*'s revelation.*) Ya'll don't think, um –

DEZ. (*With amazement.*) Faye a OG!

> (*Beat.*)
>
> (REGGIE, DEZ, *and* SHANITA *all look at each other knowingly.*)

REGGIE. It's um…it's time for everybody to get on the floor. Over these next few weeks, management is going to be looking at me a lot closer. I can't let the same ol' same ol' keep sliding by. Shanita, doctor's appointments are going to have to fit into your lunch hour or you'll have to make them after work from now on.

SHANITA. Alright.

REGGIE. And Dez, you punch in on-time or you get deducted. You understand?

DEZ. I got it.

> *(Pause. They stand in the silence, unsure of what to do. Unsure of what they are without* FAYE.*)*

REGGIE. Good then.

> *(*REGGIE *walks over to* FAYE*'s locker. Notices the pictures taped to her door are missing. He touches her locker for a moment.)*

> *(Then:)*

SHANITA. Can't believe she ain't comin' back.

> *(Resolved. Not tragic.)*

REGGIE. I know.

SHANITA. Did she do it?

REGGIE. Not all of 'em.

SHANITA. But this last job…was it her?

REGGIE. Does it matter?

DEZ. Only thing matter is if she good now. Somewhere mackin' the ladies and talkin' shit.

SHANITA. Can't imagine this place without her. *(Pause.)* She was in my dream last night. I was layin' on the shop floor, covered in dust. Floor was dusty. Walls was dusty. Everything. And I was stuck there, trying to go into labor but couldn't. And then suddenly Faye appear. Not in person, but in spirit. The dust start to write me messages and somehow I know it's her voice. I don't know how, but I just did. She write inhale. So I inhale. She write exhale. So I exhale. Then just like that, I'm breathing…in and out, and I can feel my body goin' into labor. I can feel the contractions. It all started up again. And the machines is humming. And the presses are goin'. And I'm delivering the most brilliant light I ever saw. *(Beat.)* Just when I thought I wouldn't never go back into labor, Faye show up and help me give birth.

(REGGIE opens FAYE's locker. It is empty, except for one picture taped inside. REGGIE pulls it out and looks at it. His heart swells. He flips it over and reads the back.)

(Pause.)

REGGIE. "Faye and Cathryn. Summer 1985. Love for life."

SHANITA. Who's Cathryn?

(Heartbreak and pride. It is his mother, but he is too full to speak. REGGIE looks at SHANITA but says nothing. Then, with determination.)

REGGIE. On the floor everybody. Got a full day today. Only way to get through it is to work together. Let's go.

(SHANITA and DEZ look around the room. They put their goggles on, and head out of the breakroom.)

(REGGIE stares at the room one more time. Moves into the space. Stands and closes his eyes. Inhales. Exhales.)

(Suddenly, the silhouetted workers come alive. They begin working the line. Smoothly. Collaboratively.)

(For the first time since the beginning of the play, the line has harmony.)

(Suddenly, FAYE's spirit fills the breakroom, and REGGIE can feel it. As if her name is being echoed across the lockers and the bulletin board and the floors. She becomes embedded into the soul of the plant.)

(REGGIE inhales and exhales as FAYE's spirit envelops him.)

(Lights fade on the breakroom as **REGGIE** *exits onto the floor, proudly.)*

End of Play